KU-794-970

DISPOSED OF
BY LIBRARY
HOUSE OF LORDS

THE CAREERS OF COUNCILLORS

The Careers of Councillors

Gender, party and politics

CATHERINE BOCHEL and HUGH M. BOCHEL
University of Lincolnshire and Humberside

Ashgate

Aldershot • Brookfield USA • Singapore • Sydney

Published by
Ashgate Publishing Limited
Gower House
Croft Road
Aldershot
Hampshire
GU11 3HR

Ashgate Publishing Company
Old Post Road
Brookfield
Vermont 05036
USA

Ashgate website: http://www.ashgate.com

British Library Cataloguing in Publication Data
Bochel, Catherine
The careers of councillors: gender, party and politics.
1. Local officials and employees-Great Britain. 2. Women legislators-Great Britain.
I. Title II. Bochel, Hugh M.
352. 1' 4' 0941

Library of Congress Catalog Card Number: 99-76652

ISBN 1 84014 096 8

Printed and bound by Athenaeum Press, Ltd.,
Gateshead, Tyne & Wear.

Contents

List of Tables

Preface

This book has its origins in the combination of two main areas of interest: firstly the collection of local government election results in Scotland since 1974; and secondly the belief that female councillors have different experiences, and sometimes motivations from male councillors.

The collection of local election results in Scotland has shown a continual rise in the number of women councillors (a similar pattern has also occurred in England and Wales), although to the best of our knowledge this appeared to have been more slowly reflected in the rise of women to senior positions in councils. In addition, the impression of several of those involved in collecting and analysing the election results was that there was a different pattern of electoral competition involving women candidates, for example with a feeling that there has been a greater tendency for women to fight women. Finally, whilst our initial concern was to investigate gender differences we progressed to a consideration of what we have termed councillors' 'careers' in general. It is these areas which are the concern of the research presented here, utilising a number of different sources of information in an attempt to produce a much more detailed account of councillors' careers which include and reflect party and gender differences and patterns of electoral competition and electoral success.

It is of course contestable whether the concept of a 'career' can in fact be applied to the position of local government councillors. Indeed, a small number of our survey respondents did raise this point. However, our use of the term was initially intended to denote councillors' progression through committees and to recognise that some councillors do come to be seen as more 'senior', whether through council duties or through political standing within their parties. It is also possible to argue that changes in local government over the past two decades have made the use of a 'career' concept more appropriate, including the increase in allowances for councillors, the rise of 'full-time' councillors and the greater involvement of councillors in all aspects of council work. The proposed reforms of local government by the Labour government have further added to the potential for a council 'career' becoming a reality for more councillors. This book is intended to add to this debate.

Acknowledgements

Many people have contributed to this work in a number of ways. In particular the Society of Town Clerks' Educational and Research Trust provided a small but important sum of money to allow the survey of England and Wales to progress, whilst support from the University of Lincolnshire and Humberside enabled the Scottish survey to take place. Dorothy and John Bochel provided invaluable help in the collection and inputting of data, as well as allowing us to talk ideas over with them. Finally, none of the work would have been possible without the help of the councillors themselves. Many participated through the completion of our questionnaires and a smaller number who we approached agreed to be interviewed to give a greater qualitative depth to the research. This and other research has shown the pressures of time under which many councillors operate and it is fortunate that despite this many are still willing to spend some time in helping researchers. For that we are very grateful.

1 Local Representation: Theory and Practice

The local councillors considered in this book and those who have come before and who will succeed them, are a group of citizens who unlike elected members of the European, Scottish and Westminster Parliaments, the National Assembly for Wales and the Northern Ireland Assembly, act in a largely voluntary capacity as representatives of the people. Jointly they have a long and impressive history of government of very diverse areas, from the rural districts to the major cities of the United Kingdom.

The Local Councillor in Britain

The spread of local as well as parliamentary democracy in the United Kingdom was founded on the Great Reform Act of 1832. The extension of the franchise from the 1830s created the anomalous situation of a 'democratic' House of Commons at the centre, with a wide variety of older and undemocratic forms of local administration. The pressures for change were felt particularly in the large industrial towns which were now represented in parliament but which frequently had little or no form of democratic local authority. In addition, the ideas of philosophers such as Jeremy Bentham were being taken up by political activists who sought to translate theory into practice. In his Constitutional Code (1843) Bentham had argued for a unitary state with a system of sub-national legislatures operating below the national legislature. Bentham's supporters (who came to be known as the 'Philosophic Radicals'), including Edwin Chadwick (perhaps most commonly associated with the 1848 Public Health Act, but also involved with the 1834 Poor Law Amendment Act), were amongst the most prominent campaigners for reform for direct elections by secret ballots at both national and sub-national levels. Following a Royal Commission the 1835 Municipal Corporations Act was passed, creating municipal corporations, consisting of a mixture of elected councillors and aldermen, who were selected by those councillors, in many towns and cities. In Scotland the equivalent changes had been made two years before, in 1833, again following a Royal Commission. However, in rural areas reform was delayed until the 1888 Local Government Act, which introduced the new county councils and county boroughs, again involving a mixture of elected councillors and nominated aldermen. Elected county councils were created the following year.

Although there was a gradual extension of the franchise at both national and local levels it was not until the 1945 Representation of the People Act that the franchise for local and national elections became identical. Before then the differences had primarily been related to taxation, and specifically the payment of local rates.

Where women were concerned Rallings and Thrasher's (1997a) description of the local franchise as 'a curious mix' (p. 22) of enlightened and conservative attitudes and principles is appropriate. For example, the 1818 Vestries Act gave women a vote in parish vestries, although this was withheld from married women on the grounds that their husbands would vote on their behalf. In 1869 an amendment to the Municipal Franchise Bill gave women the vote in Municipal Corporations, but a later court case restricted this to single women and excluded the wives and daughters of ratepayers. At the national level women were given the right to vote under the 1918 Representation of the People Act, although this was restricted to those aged 30 and over. Universal adult suffrage was finally introduced by the 1928 Representation of the People Act.

In terms of election to local government Hollis (1987) has charted the early years of women's activity. Among the first successes for women were elections to School Boards and Poor Law Boards. In 1870 when women were permitted to stand for the new School Boards Elizabeth Garrett headed the London school board results and two other women were elected, and from the 1880s the number of women members of School Boards and Poor Law Boards increased rapidly. From 1888 women began to contest elections to county councils and in 1889 two were elected to the London County Council, although a legal case later meant that their elections were strictly invalid and by 1891 neither was on the council. In 1895 women did become eligible to stand for rural district councils and urban district councils and immediately did so, with 140 women being elected to rural district councils that year. However, it was not until the 1907 Qualification of Women (County and Borough Councils) Act that women were finally free to contest all elected local government with the first women councillors being legally elected to town and county councils in 1910. Since then there has been a consistently steady, if unspectacular, growth in the proportion of candidates and councillors who are women in all forms of local government.

Local Democracy in Practice

The development of local democracy is closely linked with the growth of political parties. Gyford, Leach and Game (1989) have identified five stages of party political development in local government. The first, 'diversity', from 1835 to the late 1860s saw the existence of a great variety of parties which failed to meet the hopes of those who had campaigned for a democratised system of local government. The second period, 'crystallisation' lasted until the end of the nineteenth century. This saw the consolidation of local government and an expansion and greater degree of organisation within local parties. The extension of the electorate gave an incentive to develop local party organisations capable of real campaigning. In urban areas in particular there was the growth of party competition for seats, and by the end of the nineteenth century many municipal boroughs saw partisan divisions between the Conservative and Liberal Parties and were clearly controlled by one of the political parties. However, in smaller towns and rural areas 'Independents' remained dominant. The twentieth century saw 'realignment', with the established Conservative and Liberal Parties being challenged at local level by the emerging Labour Party which over forty years gradually replaced the Liberals in many parts of the country, particularly in the urban authorities. Following the Second World War there was a spell of 'nationalisation' of party politics with attempts being made to bring national and local party organisations closer together. This period also saw the continuation of the trend towards the politicisation of local government, although by the early 1970s in only just over half of councils were more than half the councillors elected with party labels (Gyford et al., 1989). The fifth stage described by Gyford et al., followed the reorganisation of local government in the mid-1970s and they termed this 'reappraisal'. During this period both Conservative and Labour Parties attempted to strengthen and extend their roles in local politics, but the principal difference was the increased stress on ideology at local level. This spell also saw a greater formalisation of party politics in the machinery of local government, with reference to party groups, meeting rooms, staffing support and other developments designed to recognise the reality of the role of parties. As discussed in Chapter 4 the 1980s and 1990s have seen a continuation of partisanship in local government with both increasing competition for seats and a decline in the proportion of Independent candidates and councillors (for example, Rallings and Thrasher, 1993; Rallings and Thrasher, 1997b; Bochel and Denver 1995). However this period also saw the continuing impact of the 'dealignment' identified by Crewe et al., (1977) at national level reflected in elections at local level, with a decline in the proportion of votes cast for the two main parties and electors' willingness to support other parties such as the Liberals, Scottish National Party and Plaid Cymru.

Democracy, Representation and Participation

The general theoretical perspectives of democracy, representation and participation lie at the heart of government in western industrialised societies, including local government. Local authorities can be seen as an important instrument of democratic self-government in that they enable participation by the ordinary citizen in the running of the local community (Parry et al., 1992). As the only form of directly elected government in Britain, other than the Westminster Parliament (prior to the Scottish Parliament and Welsh Assembly that came into being in 1999), local government played a clear role in the democratic and electoral process of the United Kingdom (the position in Northern Ireland has however been rather different). Further, entry to local politics through election to a council post is arguably more widely accessible both geographically and numerically than at national level (Hollis, 1989). For example, most people over the age of 21 are eligible to stand in local elections, although paid employees may not stand for election to their own authority. Yet, despite this, and importantly for much of the discussion in this book, councillors are generally unrepresentative of their communities, at least in socio-economic terms, so that for instance, the numbers of women local councillors have increased only gradually, representing around one-quarter of councillors in England and one-fifth of councillors in Scotland by the late 1990s. Similarly, only a very small proportion of candidates and councillors originate from ethnic minority groups.

These three concepts are clearly inter-linked and discussion of one often involves reference to the others as will be seen below.

Democracy

Democracy is normally seen as a form of rule which enables people to exercise power. Abraham Lincoln, at the time of the American Civil War, made his famous distinctions between different types of democracy when he gave a speech praising what he called 'government of the people, by the people and for the people'. This can be used to highlight the contrasting notions of democracy. For example, government by the people can be termed 'direct democracy' or 'participatory democracy'. Government for the people can be seen as a form of 'representative democracy'. Direct democracy is where the people participate in policy making and implementation. This enables citizens to rule directly without the need for professional politicians. This form of democracy is rare in the UK, but the late 1990s saw a surge in the use of direct democracy, including the Scottish, Welsh and Northern Irish referendums in 1997 and 1998. Whilst these were strictly speaking consultative, no British government has yet gone against the result of a referendum and they therefore allowed the people to vote on specific issues and thus make decisions directly.

Representative democracy is where the people elect individuals to make decisions and run affairs on their behalf, for example through the Westminster parliament and local authorities. It is of the greatest relevance to this book as it is the basis upon which local authorities are elected and which gives them legitimacy. It can be seen both as indirect and as a limited form of democracy in the sense that local councillors are elected for a specific term and the electorate only participate by voting for those people they believe will run affairs in the way they want them run. The public do not participate directly in the running of local or national affairs. Despite this, the people remain a key element in the power structure, since it is they who by casting their votes ensure democracy takes place. Representatives are seen as working in the best interests of those they represent, and are held accountable at elections when they can be removed from office by the will of the people.

Representative democracy has limitations in that it does not enable individuals to vote on individual issues and that the people have to trust their representative to act for them, but it can be argued that it is the only practicable form of democracy in a modern society, since public consultation and debate on every issue involving thousands or millions of people would simply not be a feasible way to run a country or even a local council. Any attempt at involving this number of people in the decision making process would be lengthy, result in fewer issues being dealt with and be extremely costly. In addition, it can be argued that the people as a whole lack the specialist knowledge required on each issue to make decisions in their interest as a whole (Arblaster, 1987; Heywood, 1994).

From the 1960s there has been a revival of interest in classical democracy and, in particular, the idea of participation. This has reflected growing disenchantment with the bureaucratic and unresponsive nature of modern government, as well as declining respect for professional politicians. The gradual rise in the numbers of female councillors might be seen as one feature of this since, as some of the US literature on political culture illustrates, women representatives appear to have very different priorities from their male counterparts in that they are more concerned with public welfare rather than self-promotion and enrichment (Costantini, 1990). This would also relate to the argument of some writers who also view the women's movement as a new social movement (Scott, 1990; Dalton and Knechler, 1990).

Liberal democracy is the form of democracy that has come to dominate thinking in western societies, generally as an accompaniment to the capitalist economic system (Leach, 1996). This is a form of democracy which incorporates checks and balances in the institution of government whilst at the same time respecting civil liberties and property rights. This is 'democratic' because citizens have the power to vote and thus the government are only in power through popular support. According to Heywood 'The attraction of liberal democracy is its capacity to blend élite rule with a significant measure of popular participation' (1994, p. 171). For some the perceived positive aspects of élite rule – government by experts, specialists, educated people – are balanced against accountability to citizens. In addition the existence of pressure groups acts as a further check on the power of government. There are a whole range of these groups each competing with each other to influence government. Liberal democracies are therefore sometimes described as pluralist democracies.

In summary, notions of democracy are based, to some degree, upon the idea that government can and does act in the public interest. However, there are inevitably a wide variety of criticisms of this view. For example, individualists and pluralists alike have questioned whether there is any such thing as public interest separate from the private interests of citizens. Others have doubted if there exists an electoral or constitutional mechanism through which the public interest can in practice be defined.

Drawing parallels between the 'electoral market' and other markets, some New Right thinkers (for example, Tullock, 1976 and 1988) have identified a perceived weakness in that they view politicians in the electoral market place as competing to win the support of different groups of voters. They therefore offer more and more programmes and policies, each of which can involve greater demand for resources. Public expenditure is therefore constantly under upwards pressure. From this perspective 'democracy' therefore has disadvantages. Hayek (1973), for example, has argued that whilst democracy is on balance desirable it poses dangers if not held in check.

From another part of the political spectrum, marxists also criticise liberal democracy, arguing that it is a means of legitimising capitalism. For marxists the state is seen as acting in the interests of capital and the ruling class. Control of government does not mean control of the state or the economy. Therefore the facade of elections and representative democracy are a means of suggesting to the public that they exercise power (see, for example, Miliband, 1982).

Representation

Representation has been described as 'A process in which one person or group has the capacity, usually formally established, to speak and act on behalf of a larger number of other persons or groups' (Roberts and Edwards, 1991, p. 123; see also Pitkin, 1972; Birch 1972). In the United Kingdom the two most obvious examples have been Members of Parliament at Westminster and council members who are elected to serve the local community. In politics representation creates a link between the government and the people. It implies that the interests of the people are paramount and that politicians serve as the people's representatives. Elections themselves are seen as a representative mechanism. The fact that an individual has been elected entitles them to represent the people. However, what this mandate actually means and how politicians should act is a contentious issue. For example, some have argued that it is possible for politicians to become detached from society and the people, and from the real issues and that they may end up acting only in their own selfish interests (see for example, Costantini (1990) and Bledsoe and Herring (1990) who believe that this is more likely to happen with male politicians). Thus there is a danger that representation may become a substitute for democracy.

In the United Kingdom electoral representation has been based upon the 'first past the post' system whereby the candidate to obtain the most votes wins. This system is also used in the United States. Such a system does not equate the number of seats won by each party with the number of votes cast for each party at an election. This results in large parties tending to be over-represented whilst small parties are under-represented, so that in the UK parties are regularly elected to govern with little more than two-fifths of the electorate having voted for them. With its commitment to broad constitutional reform the Labour government elected in 1997 brought a rather different approach to representation, allowing the use of one form of more proportional representation (the Additional Member system) for the elections to the Scottish Parliament and the National Assembly for Wales in 1999, another (the party list system for the 1999 European elections) and establishing the Jenkins Commission to report on electoral reform (Jenkins, 1998). A proportion electoral system, such as those used in many European countries, tends to ensure a closer relationship between the number of votes cast for each party and the number of seats obtained.

A further aspect of representation, which is of relevance to this study, is 'characteristic representation'. This suggests that representatives should be drawn from the group they are elected to represent and share its characteristics. A 'representative' government would therefore mirror the characteristics, groups and sections of society, such as social class, gender, ethnic groupings, religion and age, and in numbers that are roughly proportional to the numbers in the general population. Feminists have tended to support this notion of representation, believing that patriarchy operates to exclude women from positions in élite society and that a shift in the type of representation might produce a change. In the USA the National Organisation of Women has campaigned, alongside other groups, to improve the representation of women in areas such as politics. In the UK organisations such as the Fawcett Society and the 300 Group have pursued similar aims. At its most basic such a perspective assumes that only people drawn from a particular group can truly represent that group's interests. This however, is rather simplistic since it suggests that such representatives are incapable of, or are not amenable to listening and taking on board the views of people different from themselves. A more enlightened interpretation of this view is that representatives may empathise with the situation, plight, circumstances of a particular group of people, but not actually really appreciate what it means to be in that situation (Heywood, 1994). However, the notion of characteristic representation is not universally accepted and there are a number of weaknesses with this view. For example, a government which is effectively a microcosm of the population could be seen to reflect the very limitations and weaknesses of society and perhaps to act as a barrier to change. What is perhaps of importance from this notion is the recognition that some groups have been, and continue to be, significantly under-represented by elected representatives, one of these being women. There remains, however, a difference between those who favour parity in representation and those whose concern is the systematic under-representation of certain groups and the removal of barriers to participation.

Arising from this are a number of questions. Does representation ensure democracy and democratic government? Do representatives act in the best interests of the people? And of specific relevance to this study is the notion of characteristic representation and its implications for women, which are discussed in greater detail in Chapter 3.

Participation

The concept of participation centres attention upon the ability of individuals to take part in the democratic process. At one level this may be through voting in elections, and thus influencing government and therefore the exercise of power. At another level participation includes involvement as elected decision-makers and through being elected to take part in the democratic process of representing the local community.

Whilst there is a very substantial and wide-ranging literature on 'participation' including a great variety of forms of participation and ways of encouraging and enabling participation, for the present study it is the notion of participation in the political process which is key. Political participation can include involvement in pressure groups, political parties, voting, campaigning on behalf of particular candidates and standing for election. The term is clearly and closely associated with the notion of democracy discussed earlier. Non-democratic or undemocratic systems are generally seen as limiting participation or channelling it in particular ways.

Much of the literature on women in politics, such as that discussed later in this book, deals with issues that can be seen as hindering the participation of women in the political process, including links with the concept of representation and characteristic representation.

2 The Development of Local Government

As Hampton (1991) notes 'The origins of local government in Britain are lost not so much in the mists of time as in a fog of detail' (p. 15). Prior to the nineteenth century there was no uniform system and each municipal corporation had 'a separate and different charter; various ad hoc bodies each had their own Acts of Parliament; parish councils arose from the operation of the common law without benefit of statute; and Quarter Sessions' operated widely differing practices' (Hampton, 1991, p. 15).

The rise of capitalism and increasing industrialisation and urbanisation meant that local systems began to come under increasing pressure as large numbers of people left the land as a result of the agricultural revolution and moved into cities and towns in search of work. This frequently led to overcrowding and insanitary conditions which in turn encouraged disease and epidemics. One response to this was the creation by local or private Acts of Parliament of additional ad hoc local authority organisations. Throughout the mid-nineteenth century the growth of ad hoc bodies continued. Measures to improve sanitation, public health, highways, housing and other services were instituted on a collective basis since it was recognised that it was no longer appropriate, or in some instances possible, for the wealthy to provide services just for themselves. Disease and epidemics did not differentiate between rich and poor, making the establishment of collective services important as well as more cost effective. These services were administered at the local level because not only was this seen as more efficient, but also the 'local state' was seen to have greater knowledge of local needs and therefore to be in a better position to administer services to meet those needs.

During the twentieth century local government has continued to owe the bulk of its role to the provision of services, largely although not solely, based around the provision of welfare. Cochrane (1993) describes the 'rise of the local welfare state' as occurring in two main periods. Firstly there was a period of expansion and consolidation up to the early 1960s. During this time local government actually lost some of its powers and responsibilities as many functions became centralised, such as poor relief in 1934 and trunk roads in 1936. However, these losses were counter-balanced by the expansion of responsibilities for education and housing which came to dominate local authority budgets from the end of the Second World War to the mid-1960s. In addition, local government was arguably increasing in importance in people's everyday lives; for example, following the 1944 Education Act most children attended local authority schools until 15 and the 1947 Town and Country Planning Act meant that new development proposals had to pass through a local authority based planning system. There was also a steady growth of local authority-based personal social services, part of the 'cradle to the grave' coverage of the welfare state.

Local authorities were therefore increasingly responsible for the local management of the welfare state, dealing on a day-to-day basis with the requirements of many local people, whether they were tenants, clients or some other group. Other areas of management and service provision, seen to be 'more straightforwardly rational-bureaucratic activities' (Cochrane, 1993, p. 14) such as the distribution of social security benefits, were removed to national level, and the NHS also effectively remained outside democratic accountability, since the professional power of doctors was seen to be beyond the scope of local government. Local government was therefore the home for what Lipsky (1979) termed 'street level bureaucrats'.

Despite all these changes local government organisation remained complex with a variety of council structures, a factor which was important for Cochrane's second phase which was characterised by attempts to modernise local government. A number of reports appeared in the late 1960s and early 1970s which stressed the need for improved managerial efficiency and effectiveness within larger authorities, such as the Redcliffe-Maud (1969) and Bains (1972) reports.

It was at this time that local authority social services and social work departments emerged, together with the recognition of social workers as 'professionals'. These departments took over responsibilities that had previously been spread among children's, welfare, housing and health departments, effectively producing a new arm of the welfare state at local level.

Whilst the period up to the early 1960s had therefore been one of expansion and consolidation, from the early 1960s to the mid-1970s the emphasis was on attempts to modernise local government as part of a wider programme of state-backed social and economic modernisation, shared by governments of both major parties. However, by the mid-1970s some of the functions and operations of local government had begun to come under serious criticism, and as with other areas of the welfare state, local government's welfare role came to be affected by the notion of 'crisis'.

Administration of Services

Traditionally local authorities have played a central role in governing locally. They have had a wide range of responsibilities including refuse collection, environmental health, local planning, transport, housing, education, personal social services, and leisure, as well as fire and police services. As major providers of services used by large sections of the population they have played a central role in the community.

However, under successive Conservative governments from 1979 the service-providing functions of local authorities changed dramatically. The emphasis in many areas of operation shifted away from the provision of services towards a new role of service enablers. This function involved encouraging outside organisations, normally from the private and voluntary sectors, to become involved in service delivery, with a consequent reduction in local authority operations. Changes such as this shifted the emphasis away from day-to-day involvement in the delivery of services towards a role in overseeing service provision. This also had an impact on the degree of power and influence of local government. The changing role for local authorities was closely linked with other initiatives from the years of Conservative government, such as the emphases on marketing, cost efficiency and effectiveness, modelled in many instances upon the perceived success of the private sector in these areas and also adopted for central government.

The Structure of Local Government

The shape of local government in Britain for much of the twentieth century was established in 1929 by the Local Government Act and the Local Government (Scotland) Act. In England and Wales the boundary reviews following the Local Government Act began to tackle the problem of a large number of very small authorities. In Scotland the process of simplification was taken further with the establishment outside the four major cities of a two-tier system of two hundred district councils, 21 large burghs and 176 small burghs.

Despite these changes structural problems continued, particularly in England and Wales, resulting in further reforms in the 1960s and 1970s. Following the proposals of the Royal Commission on Local Government in Greater London the London Government Act 1963 created a two-tier structure for London with a larger Greater London Council and 32 London boroughs, the former having greater strategic responsibilities and the latter taking on the bulk of service provision, although education in inner London was made the responsibility of the Inner London Education Authority, consisting of elected councillors from the inner London boroughs. In 1966 further Royal Commissions were established for England (Redcliffe-Maud) and for Scotland (Wheatley) and both reported in 1969, the former favouring a structure of largely unitary authorities, the latter a two-tier system. However, when the Conservatives returned to power in 1970 they retained a preference for a two-tier system. The Local Government Act 1972 therefore reduced the number of county councils in England and Wales to 47 and replaced the municipal boroughs, urban and rural districts with 333 district councils. In addition 6 metropolitan counties and 36 metropolitan districts were established in the major conurbations. In Scotland the Conservatives accepted the proposals of the Wheatley Commission and the Local Government (Scotland) Act 1973 resulted in the creation of 9 regional councils, 53 district councils and 3 island councils. This remained the situation in Scotland until 1996.

The Local Government Act (Northern Ireland) 1972 established the system of local government in Northern Ireland which came into operation in October 1973. The structure consists of twenty-six unitary district councils, elected by the Single Transferable Vote (STV) system of proportional representation and based on the main centres of population. Up to the early 1970s many services were administered at the provincial level since the small size of the population made it possible to administer services in this way. Such services included water and sewerage, roads, planning, education, libraries, health, housing and welfare and childcare. However, since the suspension of the provincial parliament and its replacement by direct rule these services have been administered by departments of the Northern Ireland Government. Local democracy is therefore limited, although local government is associated with some of these services through a system of five regional boards which provide for education and library services and four for health and social services.

In England and Wales the structure of local government continued to be altered. In 1983 a White Paper, *Streamlining the Cities* (DoE, 1983), proposed the abolition of the Greater London Council and the metropolitan counties, with these being enacted in the Local Government Act 1985. This left many of their responsibilities with the London boroughs and the metropolitan districts, but others with a variety of joint boards, joint committees, ad hoc agencies and central government departments. With the abolition of the Inner London Education Authority in the Education Reform Act 1988 responsibility for education services were transferred to the inner London boroughs.

In 1991 the then Secretary of State for the Environment, Michael Heseltine, raised the prospect of further structural reorganisation of local government in a series of consultation papers. Following the 1992 general election legislation was enacted under the 1992 Local Government Act and the Local Government Commission came into being. Its remit was to review the structure of local government in England. The Commission under the chairmanship of Sir John Banham (former director-general of the Confederation of British Industry) was asked to observe two principles: to produce wherever possible, a pattern of unitary government, where people would get services from a single council; and to take account of local opinion.

Despite the pressure from the government in favour of unitary local government the Commission's recommended were mixed. It proposed that there be forty-six unitary authorities, that the status quo be retained in fourteen areas, and that twenty areas adopt a 'hybrid model', a mixture of unitary status in some parts of the county combined with two-tier status in the remainder of the area. These changes were introduced over the period from 1996 to 1998. Where unitary authorities were introduced in many instances joint boards, responsible for police and fire services, came into existence.

In Scotland the structure introduced by the 1973 Local Government (Scotland) Act remained in place until 1 April 1996 when the Local Government etc. (Scotland) Act 1994 was implemented. This introduced a new structure of 29 single tier councils to replace the structure of district and regional councils. The three island councils remained unchanged. This structure was imposed by the Secretary of State without any of the consultation or formal review process allowed for England.

The 32 councils now have all the responsibilities of the regional, district and island councils with the exceptions of reporters to Children's Panels, responsibility for which is now in the hands of the Scottish Children's Reporters Administration, and water and sewerage where three public Water Authorities have taken on this responsibility. There are also a number of joint boards or committees which administer regional services. Joint Police and Fire Board arrangements continue.

Whereas in England the Local Government Commission was created to consider proposals for re-organisation and in Scotland there was no real consultation, in Wales the Welsh Office organised its own consultation process. In 1991 a consultation paper was issued suggesting various possible 'solutions' of 13, 20 or 24 unitary authorities. A forum entitled the Welsh Consultative Council on Local Government, consisting of the Secretary of State for Wales and the Welsh Local Authority Associations, was established and assisted by the Structures group (a combination of Welsh Office civil servants and local government officers) (Cadwallader, 1995) eventually decided on 22 unitaries. On 1 April 1996, the existing eight county councils and 37 district councils were replaced by 22 unitary Authorities which assumed responsibility for all council functions. Police and Fire services were also reorganised in accordance with the new local government structure.

The Context of Local Government

In the United Kingdom local government derives its powers from central government. It is an offshoot of central government that has power to govern at the local level. Local authorities have no independent right to exist as '...all of their powers are conferred upon them by central legislation. Local government is not enshrined in the United Kingdom's uncodified constitution, and exists only at the will and discretion of Parliament. Local government can only undertake activities that have been authorised by Parliament' (Scottish Local Government Information Unit, 1995, p. 4). In recent years the powers of local government have been eroded, particularly under the Thatcher governments, who saw local authorities as bureaucratic, inefficient and contributing to excessive public expenditure (Rhodes, 1992; Stewart and Stoker, 1995; Chandler, 1996). As a result measures were introduced in order to restrict the scope of local councils to manage their own affairs, for example through the introduction of capping, contracting out and stricter central government guidance and requirements (Cochrane, 1993; Elcock, 1994; Gray, 1994). The weak constitutional position of local government is also reflected in the fact that it has undergone two major reorganisations in less than three decades.

However, until 1999, with the introduction of the Scottish Parliament, and the Welsh and Northern Ireland Assemblies, local authorities were the only form of direct representative government in Britain apart from parliament. They could therefore be seen as an instrument of democratic self-government in that they enable participation by the ordinary citizen in the running of the local community (Parry et al., 1992). In addition, is is arguably the case that for many people local politics is more accessible in both both geographical and numerical terms than is the case at national level (Hollis, 1989). In addition it can be seen as a training ground for national politicians (SLGIU, 1995; Chandler, 1996) with Norris and Lovenduski (1995) drawing on the British Candidate Survey 1992 to show that more than half of MPs had experience as local government councillors. Authorities are responsible to elected councillors who usually organise themselves along party lines. Councillors are elected from electoral divisions to stand on the council. Most people over the age of 21 are eligible to stand in local elections, although paid employees may not stand for election to the authority for which they work. In addition, the Local Government and Housing Act 1989 prevents local government employees above a certain grade or in jobs deemed to be politically sensitive from taking part in political activities including canvassing for a political party or standing for local or national elections.

Gray and Jenkins (1994) have discussed the way in which political differences within councils were accommodated within the normal structures and procedures under the traditional model of council workings and how these began to come under strain in the early 1980s causing the Conservative government concern. As a result the government set up the Widdicombe Committee (1986a) to examine *inter-alia* the rights and responsibilities of elected members and to suggest ways to strengthen the democratic process. The report strongly favoured local elected officials making decisions and recognised that political organisation in local government was inevitable and that politics was '...now the main determining factor in the decisions of most local authorities' (p. 62) and that this should be recognised and accommodated. Furthermore, it acknowledged the role and importance of central government in setting the framework for local politics, but argued that, if local government was truly to be *local*, it would reflect local as opposed to national demands, and if it was really *government*, then political tensions with the centre would be inevitable. However, the government effectively ignored that area of the report's findings and limited its response to issues that fitted with its own wider vision, in particular limiting the political activities of council employees (Gray and Jenkins, 1994). The majority of the proposals from the white paper (Department of the Environment et al., 1988) were eventually incorporated into the Local Government Act 1989.

Electoral Patterns

Until the 1970s much of local politics was non-partisan in the sense that many councillors did not represent political parties (Elcock, 1994). In addition there were substantial numbers of uncontested divisions. However, 'since 1974, local politics has become much more partisan and ... this includes a much greater tendency for party groups to vote cohesively' (Widdicombe, 1986a, p. 60; also see Gray and Jenkins, 1994). For example, Bochel and Denver (various years) have illustrated the growth in partisanship in Scotland. Since 1974 this has led to an increase both in the number of seats contested and an increase in the number of three and four way contests between the major parties (Labour, Conservative, Liberal Democrats, Scottish Nationalists) (Bochel and Denver, various years). Similar patterns can be identified in England and to a lesser extent in Wales so that Rallings and Thrasher (1997a) have been able to state that 'Local politics is now largely about party politics... Local elections have become party politicised to the extent that a smaller and smaller proportion of contests now feature only 'Independent' or minor party candidates... Party politics has not quite taken over local government, but each cycle of elections and each structural change increases its grip' (pp. 99-100).

There have also been changing patterns of party support. In England there has been considerable fluctuation, as evidenced in the case of the shire counties (Table 2.1). Rallings and Thrasher (1997a) note a weakening in support for the two major parties across the different types of local authority in England together with the rise of the Liberal Democrats. In addition with the growth of partisanship in local government support for

Independents fell rapidly and from the 1980s their role has been highly marginal.

Table 2.1 Share of vote in English shire counties 1973-97 (%)

	1973	1977	1981	1985	1989	1993	1997
Conservative	42.1	58.1	40.7	38.4	42.2	35.6	36.9
Labour	37.6	25.9	34.8	30.0	31.1	31.2	32.2
Liberal/Alliance	9.2	8.7	18.3	27.9	20.2	29.3	26.8
Independent	9.1	4.5	3.5	2.5	2.0	1.8	2.6
Other	2.0	2.9	2.7	1.2	4.5	2.2	1.5

Source: Rallings, C. and Thrasher, M. (1997a) *Local Elections in Britain*, Routledge, London, p. 113 and Rallings, C. and Thrasher, M. (1997b) *Local Elections Handbook 1997*, Local Government Chronicle Elections Centre, Plymouth, p. vi.

Since 1974 Labour have become the dominant party in much of Scotland with fluctuating increases in Scottish National Party (SNP) and Liberal Democrat support and Conservative and Independent decline. For example, in the regions in 1974 there were 114 Independent councillors (Bochel and Denver, 1974) and by 1994 this had fallen to 65 (Bochel and Denver, 1994). In the districts in 1974 there were 345 Independent councillors (Bochel and Denver, 1974) and by 1992 this had fallen to 228 (Bochel and Denver, 1992).

Table 2.2 illustrates the share of the votes obtained by each party in the most recent elections for each tier from 1992 to 1995. In each case Labour have the largest share of the vote followed by the SNP who remain stable with approximately a one-quarter share of the vote. The Conservatives are in third place and the Liberal Democrats fourth.

In Wales too Labour's dominance grew over the 1980s and into the 1990s. However, in other respects voting patterns in local elections have differed from Scotland. The Conservatives have not displayed any significant strength for more than two decades, whilst the tradition of support for Independent candidates, although weakening, has remained strong. Rallings and Thrasher (1997a) note that Independent candidates have never polled below one-quarter of the vote in Welsh district elections, although the drift towards partisanship has been more marked in the counties.

Table 2.2 Share of votes in Scottish local elections 1992-95 (%)

	District elections 1992	Regional elections 1994	Council elections 1995
Con	23.2	13.7	11.3
Lab	34.1	41.8	43.8
Lib Dem	9.5	11.9	9.7
SNP	24.3	26.8	26.2
Ind	7.4	4.2	7.6
Other	1.9	1.1	1.5

Source: Bochel, H. M. and Denver, D. T. (1995) *Scottish Council Elections: Results and Statistics*, p. vii, Election Studies, Newport on Tay: Fife.

Trends in Women's Participation

An analysis of the pattern of elections over the period since the last reorganisations of local government shows that there has been a clear trend towards increasing participation by women, both as candidates and as councillors. Rallings and Thrasher (1997a) have illustrated that there has been a continuous increase in England and have analysed a number of possible reasons for this (see Chapter 4) whilst Bochel and Denver (various years) have charted the change in Scotland. In the Scottish districts the percentage of women candidates increased from 14 per cent in 1974 to 27 per cent in 1992 with the percentage of councillors rising from 13 per cent to 22 per cent; for regions the increase in women candidates was from 12 per cent to 22 per cent and in women councillors from 10 per cent to 17 per cent. These figures show that the growth in the proportion of councillors is lower than the growth in the proportion of candidates, a finding repeated in Rallings and Thrasher's (1997a) analysis of the English shire counties. Bochel and Denver cite as possible reasons for this that 'women are candidates for the less successful parties', and that they also 'appear to fight less promising seats than men whatever the party they represent' (1992, pp. ii-iii) whilst Rallings and Thrasher (1997a) suggest that 'in the eyes of voters at least, gender is not an issue in selecting councillors' (p. 77) but that other factors account for these discrepancies. These issues are pursued in greater depth in Chapters 3 and 4.

Councillors

Since the 1960s there have been many studies of local government councillors in the United Kingdom. The focus of these has varied widely to include areas such as recruitment, including candidate selection and electoral discrimination; gender, and particularly the under-representation of women on local councils; operation; structure; ideology and attitudes; turnover; workload; constraints of private life on participation; and the social characteristics of council members. This section reviews some of this literature in the light of the relevance for the study of councillors' 'careers'.

Roles and Responsibilities

Councils fulfill an executive function in that they implement legislation and policies made by central government, although they also make policies which may be contrary to those of central government (John, 1990; Rhodes, 1992; Stewart and Stoker, 1995). As a group councillors are responsible for ensuring that the statutory duties of the local authority are fulfilled. In theory, they decide which policies a council should pursue and then the officers of the council implement those policies. In practice, this relationship is less straightforward. Councillors look to the salaried officers of the local authority to provide them with information and to provide advice on the options open to them and thus the outcome is often polices decided on the basis of input from both officers and councillors (Gray and Jenkins, 1994; SLGIU, 1995; Chandler, 1996).

Political groupings are now important in most councils. They were recognised in England and Wales by the Local Government and Housing Act 1989 which gave them specific rights, such as committee representation and the right to appoint political assistants. Whilst no statutory instrument has been introduced in Scotland most councils have nevertheless followed the principles of the Act. In general, party groups determine their own policies including in many instances the production of local manifestoes, and also tend to meet before council meetings to decide the position they will adopt on specific issues and agenda items (Hampton, 1991; Elcock, 1994; Chandler, 1996). Where a party has an overall majority the decision of the ruling party group will generally effectively decide the position of the council. Party discipline is therefore an important factor in the effectiveness of party groupings. Chandler (1996) notes that 'A group whip has the task, like the House of Commons equivalent, of informing members of their strategy in any debate, monitoring how colleagues vote and, in consultation with other senior party members, instituting disciplinary procedures should a member fail to follow the party line' (p. 152).

The full council, when it meets, is a powerful body, although the existence of party groups within this, and the way in which they exercise their power, will affect the ability of the full council to act on issues. Cooperation between parties and discipline within parties is the key to this. All council members have the right to vote. The full council meets at regular intervals. However, because there is an enormous volume of council business much of which is complex, it is necessary to delegate powers to council committees. These committees have the power to delegate to sub-committees or to officials and have the authority of the full council (Gray and Jenkins, 1994; SLGIU, 1995). Local authorities are not required to appoint committees except for certain purposes (education, social services and police, where these are applicable). There are a wide range and variety of committees but they can broadly be classified as either 'service' or 'resource' committees. Service committees determine policy and are responsible for monitoring service delivery, such as housing, education, social services (England and Wales) or social work (Scotland) and environmental health. Resource committees tend to deal with council wide issues which are not specific to any one area of council business. Examples include finance and personnel. The most important committee is generally Policy and Resources, although this may have different names according to the authority, the role of which is to formulate general policy and objectives. Very small councils may not have separate committees.

The division into committees enables members to specialise in particular areas and to develop knowledge or apply existing expertise to a particular area (Elcock, 1994). Most councillors will serve on some committees. In England and Wales representation on committees is required to reflect the political balance of the council. In Scotland this is normally the case although there is no statutory requirement for this.

The chair of each committee has an important role in agenda setting and liaising with the chief officer of the council (Elcock, 1994). They often exert considerable influence over their area of responsibility. Similarly holders of senior council positions such as chairs, leaders or convenors (in Scotland) can also wield significant power (Chandler, 1996). However, it is important to note that each authority determines committee structures and senior posts and that the power and influence of these positions may vary widely. Similarly, leaders of the largest party groups, who may not hold a formal council title, also have potentially powerful roles.

The traditional committee system has come under criticism for a variety of reasons. For example, the Scottish Local Government Information Unit, in its *Guide to Scottish Local Government*, highlights a number of criticisms of the traditional committee system: 'stifling debate; focusing on service provision rather than long term policy strategies; compartmentalising discussions; seldom providing opportunities for members to consider service provision in a corporate way; and, emphasising input from chief officials and limiting the management responsibility of staff in less senior positions' (1995, p. 49). In the light of these criticisms a number of councils have introduced reforms such as working parties and seminars to explore issues, more open styles of decision-making involving wider consultation with the public and attempts to increase their participation, and councillor-officer working parties to explore specific issues. Within a year of taking office in 1997 the Labour government gave notice of its concerns with these and other aspects of the workings of local government in England and Wales through consultation papers such as *Modernising local government: Local democracy and community leadership* (DETR, 1998a) whilst in Scotland the remit of the Commission on the Scottish Parliament and Local Government also included consideration of some of these issues.

In addition to serving on committees, councillors have another major role in that they act as representatives of their constituents. This may involve dealing with electors' problems and queries, public consultation and meeting external organisations (Young and Rao, 1994). This can be time consuming and generate much administration. The various duties of councillors mean that many have a heavy workload – an area of research that has been well documented. The Widdicombe commission (1986a) found that councillors in Scotland spent an average of 102 hours per month on council business and attending council meetings, those in Wales 80 hours and English councillors 72, with significant differences also between types of authority. In 1995 a SLGIU/Scottish Local Authorities Management Centre survey found that the average councillor in Scotland anticipated spending between 31 and 40 hours a week on council business (SLGIU, 1995b) although other estimates vary widely, with some being much higher (for example, see Maud, 1964; Robinson, 1976; Barron, 1990; and Young and Rao, 1994). The proportion of time councillors spend on their duties obviously impacts on full-time employment outside their local councillor posts and on their financial situation.

Remuneration

Remuneration is important because it is arguably a significant factor affecting peoples' ability to fulfill the role of councillor, particularly with the growth in local government responsibilities. Robinson (1977) and Widdicombe (1986a) were concerned that surveys showed that a majority of councillors were in full-time employment and that they might suffer financially through loss of earnings during their absences. Research undertaken by Young and Rao (1994) illustrated that in 1993 32 per cent of councillors worked full-time and 19 per cent were self-employed. Similarly those councillors who are not in any paid employment may face financial hardship.

Remuneration is also an important feature if, in some instances at least, local government service is seen in terms of a 'career'. With the growth in partisanship and an apparent increase in full-time councillors (discussed in Chapters 4 and 5) methods of remuneration to councillors may become increasingly important.

Prior to the Local Government Act 1948, there was no uniform system of payments to councillors and councils only had very limited powers in this area. Hampton, referring to the Robinson Commission (1977) notes that only Scottish county councils could pay their members any allowances for the time taken off from their ordinary employment to attend council business (1991), although no remuneration was available for chairmen or provosts in Scottish councils. The 1948 Act established two principles: that '...council members should be eligible to receive payments for loss of earnings or necessary expenses; and that these payments should relate to the performance of "approved duties"' (Hampton, 1991, p. 123) a system that continued with only slight amendments until the 1970s. In 1972 in England and Wales and in 1973 in Scotland a system of attendance allowances was introduced to which councillors were entitled as of right, without the need to demonstrate financial loss, for the performance of duties approved by the local authority. In 1980 the Local Government Planning and Land Act gave councillors the choice between the two systems of allowances: loss of earnings allowance or attendance allowance.

An ad hoc system of allowances has therefore existed which has aimed to enable councillors to fulfill their duties. Councillors have not been paid a salary, although the Wheatley Commission (1969) was in favour of such an approach for Scotland. From 1990 a new system of councillor remuneration was introduced which operated similarly in England and Wales and Scotland. This had three main elements. Firstly, the Secretary of State had to decide on the maximum sum a council in a given population band could spend on allowances. Secondly, councils had to decide how much of the total could be spent on special responsibility allowances paid to leading councillors, such as council leaders and other specific posts. A limit was also set for the maximum figure any single councillor could receive. And finally, each council had to use a proportion of its total to pay a basic flat rate allowance to each councillor. The remainder could be used to pay an attendance allowance. In Scotland, with the introduction of the new councils in 1996, the Minister of State has accepted a proposal for a new system to give councils 'discretion as to the number and level of special responsibility allowances' with the Convention of Scottish Local Authorities (CoSLA) providing guidance on the level of such allowances (CoSLA, 1996, p. 3).

Making councillors full-time politicians, as is sometimes proposed, would alter the nature of the councillors role. It might affect the numbers of people standing for the council, the fundamental nature of the relationship between councillors and officers would change and it could be expensive. Nevertheless, the issue of remuneration continues to be of importance and under the Labour government again received attention including in England and Wales through the consultation paper *Modernising local government: Local democracy and community leadership* (DETR, 1998a) and in Scotland through the Commission on Local Government and the Scottish Parliament (CLGSP, 1998).

Characteristics

There already exists a substantial literature covering a wide range of areas of research on local government councillors. The literature highlights the complex roles and responsibilities of councillors, often compounded by the structure and operation of councils – the often inflexible working arrangements, issues such as the power structure within councils, attitudes towards women councillors, remuneration and workload. Furthermore, the fact that councillors are unrepresentative of the population as a whole underlines an equal opportunities issue across gender, race and class. Councillors throughout the United Kingdom tend to be sociologically unrepresentative of the population, being disproportionately male, middle-class, middle-aged, homeowners, be educated to college or university standard and have previous experience of being councillors. A number of major national surveys on local government have been conducted – the Maud Committee (1967), Robinson Committee (1977) and the Widdicombe Committee (1986a). These, *inter-alia* considered the personal characteristics and background of councillors to find out whether they were representative of the population as a whole. Despite spanning a twenty year period the findings of these reports were remarkably similar and Widdicombe noted that 'Elected members as a group are still highly unrepresentative of the overall population' (1986b, p. 19). Tables 2.3 and 2.4 illustrate the position in 1985, when the research for the Widdicombe Report was undertaken. That the position remains largely unchanged has been reflected in more recent research, such as that of Cadwallader (1995), SLGIU (1995a) and LGMB (1997).

Table 2.3 Councillors and population by gender, 1985 (%)

	Councillors	Population
Male	81	49
Female	19	51

Source: Widdicombe Committee (1986b) Committee of Inquiry into the Conduct of Local Authority Business: Research Vol. II, *The Local Government Councillor*, HMSO, London.

Table 2.4 Councillors and population by age, 1985 (%)

	Councillors	Population
Up to 24	0	12
25 to 34	7	20
35 to 44	19	19
45 to 54	25	16
55 to 59	13	8
60 to 64	14	8
65 to 74	19	11
75 and over	3	6

Source: Widdicombe Committee (1986b) Committee of Inquiry into the Conduct of Local Authority Business: Research Vol. II, *The Local Government Councillor*, HMSO, London.

For the purposes of this book, one of the major disparities at local government level, as well as at Westminster, is the continued under-representation of women, and this is discussed in detail in Chapter 3. In addition, other 'minority groups', such as ethnic minorities and disabled people, also appear to be under-represented throughout elected government in the United Kingdom, although there is at present very little information available upon which to base sound judgements. Despite this, on the basis of available data, Rallings and Thrasher (1997a) do note that 'Councillors appear to reflect the population from which they are drawn better in the case of the Asian than the Black community' (p. 78) and that in some authorities Asian communities are 'over-represented'. Nevertheless, national surveys, such as that by the Local Government Management Board (1997) find that they under-represented as a whole.

The Management of Local Authorities

There have also been government considerations of the internal management of local authorities which have impacted upon councillors. Where this was concerned the Widdecombe Committee accepted the existing model of decision-making, although recommending some changes such as the composition of committees and subcommittees with delegated powers to reflect the political balance of the council (whilst at the same time recognising that the reality of party politics meant that in many authorities the important decisions were made in party groups and formalised in the council or committees) and thus recommending allowing deliberative committees to be composed only of members from one party and also excluding them from the right of the press and public to attend under the Local Government (Access to Information) Act 1995. However, whilst accepting the recommendation on committees with delegated powers the government argued that balanced composition should also apply to deliberative committees and that these should not be exempted from the requirements of the Local Government (Access to Information) Act 1995 (Stewart, 1995).

Following the Widdecombe Report the Conservative Government enacted the Local Government and Housing Act 1987 but in 1989 the new Secretary of State, Michael Heseltine, produced a consultation paper (DoE, 1989) which suggested further changes for England and Wales, and, in contrast to many of the other changes affecting local government made by the Conservatives, suggested piloting in a small number of authorities. The emphasis in this consultation paper was on ways of improving decision-making in local government, and unlike the Widdecombe report it put forward a number of radical options with significant implications for councillors: an appointed collective executive – a 'cabinet' system; an elected collective executive; an elective individual executive – an 'elected mayor'.

The consultation paper recognised that these approaches would involve a small number of elected representatives taking on significantly enhanced roles and argued that there was therefore a case for considering whether these posts should be on a salaried basis.

Following consultation, another Secretary of State, Michael Howard, set up a departmental working party, with a membership largely drawn from local authority associations and others familiar with local government (Stewart, 1995). The Working Party's report (Working Party on the Internal Management of Local Authorities, 1993) identified two major objectives: to strengthen the role of all elected members and to develop the framework for effective leadership within local authorities. It recognised the extent of change which had already occurred in many authorities and the diversity of forms which the new decision-making mechanisms took, identifying three main directions: the restructuring of committee systems; the development of policy and performance review panels; devolution of responsibility, including the creation of area committees.

Whilst the Working Party called upon local authorities to review their internal management arrangements it did not recommend any general change in legislation to encourage or enable this. The only general change came in the recommendation on the rules governing councillors' allowances where it proposed: giving local authorities greater discretion over what allowances to pay and to whom, with the government specifying only a minimum basic allowance to be paid to all councillors; removing the upper limit on the payment of special responsibility allowances; making specified party meetings and single member duties eligible for payment of allowances.

It argued that wider changes should wait for the results of experimentation. The Working Party argued that any developments should develop by a process of evolution from existing systems and experience and set out four models of political executive:

1) the single party executive committee, where decisions taken by the executive would become decisions of the council, although councils could reserve some powers and functions to full council or committees and the executive's decisions could be challenged and/or vetoed;

2) a lead member system, with the council delegating executive powers to named lead members, rather than to a collective political executive. Lead members could form a non-executive committee with individuals then having individual executive powers to carry out the policies agreed in their meetings. Committees could still operate, but would be for scrutiny rather than executive purposes;

3) a cabinet system, with a single party policy committee having individual and combined executive powers. Decisions by the executive would be decisions of the council. Individual members would have delegated areas of responsibility but broad strategy would be determined by the executive;

4) a strong political executive – a separate legal entity, where a separate executive, drawn from the council membership, would have its own legal powers and status and would control the decision taking process on behalf of the council.

The Working Party proposed that there be legislation allowing local authorities to experiment with their internal management structures, to be approved by the Secretary of State.

Whilst there were no further changes under the Conservatives the Labour government, elected in 1997 did produce new proposals for change, with substantial elements based upon these discussions.

'Careers'

One of the concerns of this book is the 'careers' of councillors. There are clearly a number of possible uses of the term 'career', however at present it is used here not in the sense of a job, but primarily as a way of describing people's experience as councillors over their period in office. This reflects the situation that for many councillors there is a sense of progression, usually from being a newly elected junior councillor to positions of greater authority and power (and perhaps back to less senior positions again) and perhaps through a hierarchy of committees. It is of course debatable to what extent different interpretations of the concept of a 'career' can actually be applied to the position of local government councillors, and this is considered in Chapters 4 and 5. Nevertheless, at a minimum the concept does provide one approach to examining councillors' motivations, experiences and ambitions and might serve to link otherwise disparate pieces of research and elements of council service. In addition there are other factors which may make the use of the term more apposite, such as the extent to which an increasing number of councillors appear to be in some sense 'full-time'. This discussion will continue to encompass key issues from this Chapter, such as selection, political ambitions, remuneration and gender differences, and analyse whether these appear to have any relationship to the way in which councillors 'careers' develop over time.

Proposals for Reform

Following Labour's return to government in 1997 the Department of the Environment, Transport and the Regions published a consultation paper (DETR, 1998a) setting out an agenda for 'democratic renewal' for local government in England. This set out four broad areas for change:

1) modernising electoral arrangements to improve the accountability of councils and to increase participation in local elections;

2) developing new ways in which councils can listen to their communities and involve local people in their decisions, and in their policy planning and review;

3) devising new ways of working for councils, giving them clearer political and management structures;

4) strengthening councils' role as leaders of their local communities, by reinforcing their existing potential for local leadership, and by developing a new framework in which councils having the support of their communities can be given the powers they need to meet the priorities and aspirations of those communities.

In the subsequent white paper *Modern Local Government: In Touch with the People* (DETR, 1998b) these ideas were taken a stage further with proposals which included:

- changes to political management structures based upon one of three models which separates the executive from the backbench role of elected councillors – a directly elected mayor with a cabinet, a cabinet with a leader, or a directly elected mayor and a council manager;

- annual election of councillors by thirds, together with the use of referendums to consult the people and the possibility of new and more accessible approaches to enabling voting;

- greater emphasis on ethical standards and frameworks within local authorities, including for councillors.

In Scotland Labour's approach to local government was further complicated by the creation of the Scottish Parliament. A Commission on Local Government and the Scottish Parliament (Mackintosh Commission) was set up:

> to consider how to build the most effective relations between local government and the Scottish Parliament and the Scottish Executive; and
>
> to consider how councils can best make themselves responsive and democratically accountable to the communities they serve.
>
> Scottish Office (1998a) *The Commission on Local Government and the Scottish Parliament: Consultation Paper 1*, The Stationery Office, London, p. 3

The modernisation of local government in Scotland was taken up in the Commission's first consultation paper (Scottish Office, 1998). Again the emphasis was on a more open and participative approach to resolving some of the key issues facing local democracy ranging from the recruitment of local councillors and the qualities required in elected members, to the operation of councils, the committee system and the ability and effectiveness of local councils to consult local communities and effect local democracy. In it's final report the Commission (Commission on Local Government and the Scottish Parliament, 1999) made a number of recommendations pertinent to the concerns of this book with some significant differences from those outlined for England including:

- a four year term with elections taking place at the mid-point of the Scottish Parliament's term;

- the use of proportional representation for elections to local government;

- that councils review their methods of political decision-making paying particular concern to executive models and simplification of committee systems;

- that all councils produce job descriptions for their members and that a pay and conditions package for councillors should be drawn up, including topics such as superannuation, childcare provision and allowances, but that for most councillors a basic allowance should be retained rather than a salary paid;

- the replacement of Special Responsibility Allowances with salaries for those councillors with the heaviest responsibilities;

- ending the existing blanket ban on employees being members of the councils which employs them, but retaining safeguards to ensure that senior officers and those in politically sensitive posts cannot be elected.

Labour's constitutional and governmental reforms clearly have the potential for significant impact on the 'careers' of councillors, from election, through to the mode of operation and to the ability of councillors to respond to the concerns of their constituents. The emphasis in approach has shifted from a primarily market-led one under the previous Conservative administrations to an apparently more open, participative and democratically accountable one under new Labour. However, the ultimate outcome and its implications for local government and elected councillors may not be clear for some time.

3 Local Government and the Representation of Women

The relatively low numbers of women in local government, whether it be referred to in terms of problems of recruitment or under-representation, has been apparent throughout the twentieth century, not just in the United Kingdom but in many other countries. A variety of explanations have been put forward for this including discrimination by electors and selectors, a failure on the part of women to present themselves for election and the barriers that discourage women from standing. Yet despite this it is apparent that from the 1970s there has been an increase in the proportion of candidates and councillors who are women. Bochel and Denver (for example, 1992, 1994 and 1995) and Rallings and Thrasher (for example, 1997b) have charted these increases for Scotland and England and Wales respectively. In addition, research undertaken by Young and Rao (1994) in England, Scotland and Wales also found that important changes had taken place in respect of councillors' representation in leadership positions. Their results indicated that women were now proportionately as likely as men to hold senior council positions.

Hollis (1989) has argued that women have done better in local rather than parliamentary politics for a number of reasons: they have found it hard to obtain safe parliamentary seats; Westminster may be more distant from home and family whilst local government is inevitably more local, making it easier to integrate the potential demands of family, work and political life; local government is more accessible, with more seats and less competition for them; local government is less intimidating than central government and power is more widely diffused; and local government has become more open to women with more women seeking election, the promotion of equal opportunities for women staff and women's issues more firmly on the agenda.

Women, Parties and Representation

Historically the under-representation of women in local and even national politics was not always an issue of importance. For many feminists 'The extent of women's participation in formal political institutions was at best seen as an irrelevance and at worst as the propping-up of institutions which were in themselves repressive' (Lindsay, 1991, p. 7). However, '...it gradually became clear nothing was going to change unless power was challenged – only those who sat at the table would get a slice of the cake' (Coote and Patullo, 1990, cited in Lindsay, 1991, p. 8). By the 1970s and 1980s many areas of politics were being affected by new consciousness and debate over the politics of gender and to some extent race. One field where this was particularly true was the under-representation of women in political élites and in decision-making. In 1980 the all-party 300 Group was formed with the aim of seeing the election of 300 women MPs to the House of Commons before the year 2000. However, it quickly became clear that this would not be achieved and many women chose to campaign for change within the individual parties. The Liberal Democrats have frequently fielded the largest proportion of women candidates in both local and national elections, but have failed to get large numbers elected to parliament. Whilst lagging behind the Liberal Democrats in encouraging women to stand at local level, the Labour Party in the 1980s and 1990s gradually moved towards a form of positive discrimination for parliamentary elections, which although found to be in breach of the law in 1996, did nevertheless result in the number of women Labour MPs increasing to 101 at the 1997 general election. The Conservatives have arguably been the slowest of the major parties at addressing the issue, and it was only after their crushing defeat in 1997 that the new party chairman, Archie Norman, was able to attempt to raise the prospect of bringing his party more into line with Labour and Liberal Democrats.

In Scotland, arguably even more than in the rest of the UK, the debate on constitutional change in the 1980s and 1990s added further impetus to the issue of women's representation in public life. The establishment of the Scottish Constitutional Convention in 1989 to agree a scheme for a future Scottish Parliament marked a change in attitude. The Women's Movement was represented on this and one of the groups set up by the Convention was the Women's Issues Group. This was given the remit to devise ways of improving the representation of women in a Scottish Parliament. This marked a significant shift from the lack of interest in women's representation which had prevailed a decade earlier. Parallel to these developments, A Woman's Claim of Right group (AWCR) was formed in protest at the small proportion of women (ten per cent) nominated for membership of the Scottish Constitutional Convention. This group comprised women from different political parties as well as those who were not formally involved in politics. AWCR set themselves the task of monitoring the work of the Convention and its likely implications for women. From 1987 Brown (1996) argues that a 'Third Wave of Feminism' (p. 41) took place in Scotland and can be seen to be linked to campaigns for constitutional reform. This move saw women in different political parties, groups and organisations working together, to improve the representation of women.

Women's demands for political representation are part of a two-way process. The structure of political parties, their ideology and their mode of operation will affect the type of strategies women employ to gain greater representation. At the same time the demands from women will impact on political parties (Lovenduski, 1993). This is arguably of particular importance given the links with the feminist concept of 'the personal is political' (Butler and Scott, 1992; Grant, 1993) in that the issues affecting women cannot be seen to remain in the private sphere, but have transference into the political arena. The process of negotiation over such demands will result in mutual adjustments by both sides in the policy-making process. Lovenduski refers to the need to '...consider both the programmatic and the organizational dimensions of representation: how parties differ in their treatment of women's issues and in their strategies to promote women's representation' (1993, p. 6). Political parties have generally taken on board women's issues and demands to a greater or lesser extent. These *inter-alia* include the adoption of equal opportunities strategies and polices within the party, commitment to equal pay in the workplace, and the adoption of particular stances on specific issues such as family policy. This has largely been done in order to appeal to women members and voters. However, the way in which this has been undertaken differs according to political ideology. For example, under the Conservative governments from 1979 to 1997 women were frequently promoted in terms of their family caring role, underpinning a traditional right-wing ideological viewpoint, whilst under Labour from 1997, women and particularly single mothers have been seen as a labour resource, with employment both being an economic good and giving women more independence and control over their own lives. In respect of organizational change, parties have developed ways of increasing the proportion of women in positions in the decision-making process. Lovenduski (1993) sees these as falling into three broad categories. The first, 'rhetorical strategies' may involve frequent reference to the importance of getting more women elected, in speeches, campaign materials and so on. She notes however that 'A commitment to women's representation in party rhetoric may be the beginning of a process that will lead to more substantial policies of inclusion' (p. 8). The second is positive or affirmative action including training and sometimes financial assistance, for example through Emily's List encouraging and enabling women to become candidates for the Labour Party. Similarly, at the 1997 Liberal Democrat Conference a woman delegate reiterated the importance of such a strategy supporting 'a fund to help potential candidates...' as this would be important in boosting confidence and providing practical help as well as training and support (*The Guardian*, 23 September 1997). The final strategy is that of positive discrimination. This may include reserving places for women, for example on shortlists or on decision-making bodies. One example of this was the quotas for women agreed by the Labour Party in 1993 (Squires, 1996), involving drawing up all-women shortlists in half the marginal and vacant seats for the next general election. However, this approach was later abandoned following a successful legal challenge. Reflecting the Liberal Democrats' continued failure to return significant numbers of female MPs, a proposal to the 1997 conference, despite fears of a legal challenge, wanted to ensure that half of all shortlisted candidates for the Westminster and European Parliaments were women; however this move was defeated. Similarly, at one stage Labour, Liberal Democrats and Scottish National Parties were hoping to achieve equal representation of women in the Scottish Parliament in 1999 using similar measures, but the legality of methods of achieving this was in doubt.

Explaining Women's Under-Representation

From the mid-1970s there has been a slow but steady growth in the number of women elected to both parliament and local government. The numbers of women elected to the Westminster parliament rose gradually from 22 in 1974 to 57 at the 1992 general election, with the major increase to 114 coming at the 1997 general election, following which women made up 18 per cent of Members of Parliament. Within local government the pattern was broadly similar, with the proportion of councillors who were women reaching 28 per cent for the London boroughs in 1994 and the English shire districts in 1995, although only 22 per cent of successful candidates in the metropolitan boroughs in 1994 were women (Rallings and Thrasher, 1997a). In Scotland there was an increase at district level from 12 per cent in 1974 to 22 per cent in 1992 and from 10 to 17 per cent at the regional level in 1994. The elections for the new councils in 1995 saw 26 per cent of councillors being women (Bochel and Denver, 1992, 1994 and 1995). In Wales women were only 19 per cent of councillors in 1995 (Rallings and Thrasher, 1997a).

Numerous studies have been undertaken which document the under-representation of women in local (and national) politics and a wide variety of explanations have been propounded including discrimination on the part of selectors that prevents women from getting nominated for winnable seats, that voters do not believe that women can hold down top political posts, that women will not vote for women; and that women candidates cannot raise the same level of resources (Seltzer, Newman and Leighton, 1997). The remainder of this Chapter explores some of these explanations and applies them to the situation in Britain.

It is difficult to categorise the numerous explanations put forward to try and explain the under-representation of women in elected politics because there is significant overlap between both these 'theories' and the data upon which they are built. For the purposes of this book we have divided the discussion primarily into consideration of what might loosely be termed 'individual' (or in some cases even 'personal') explanations and 'structural' or 'system' explanations. However, even with such a basic categorisation there are some interpretations which overlap and others which do not easily fit into either group.

Individual Circumstances and Personal Characteristics

The particular theories or explanations subsumed under this heading include family responsibilities and commitments, family support, individual circumstances, for example life-style, availability of and control over financial resources, social class background, educational qualifications, political ambition, experience of work outside the home and psychological factors such as confidence and self-esteem. Many of these can be seen as holding women back from standing for election giving a clear link with what are often described as 'supply' explanations.

Bristow (1980) puts forward an explanation for the under-representation of women in local government based on social class. He states 'It is clear that the level of women's representation is most closely associated with both affluence and Conservatism' (p. 82). This is explained partly on the basis that in affluent areas there are greater numbers of women 'available for public service' who do not need to work for financial remuneration. It can also be explained by the different recruitment methods used by the political parties which '...helps to reinforce the lower levels of involvement of women in the less affluent areas' (p. 83). According to Bristow this is linked to women's involvement in voluntary work. The Conservative Party tends to approach women through this avenue, whereas the Labour Party tend to select councillors from a panel of candidates after they have become active within other areas of the party. He concluded that 'Insofar as women are frequently active in local voluntary associations..., they are more likely to be approached by representatives of the Conservative Party than of the Labour Party with an invitation to stand' (p. 84). However, with changing patterns of women's participation and parties' attitudes this may arguably be reversed in the 1990s. Sharp (1991) considers Bristow's explanation in relation to Scotland and concedes that the affluence of an area may make a difference to women's participation in Scotland citing evidence which she believes makes such a theory credible. However, she recognises that further research is necessary if this explanation is to be given broader acceptance. Even so, it does not explain the key question of why so few women put themselves forward for election to local councils.

Hills (1982) introduces lifestyle factors into the debate, arguing that these '...continue to play a part in determining whether women are available for formal political recruitment' (p. 70). She notes that it is impossible to separate women's private lives from any role they may undertake involving public participation and concedes that Bristow (1980), whom she criticises for his emphasis on social class as a factor in the recruitment of women candidates, '...may yet be proved right and the only women with the resources to enter politics may come to be housewives who are middle class and financially secure' (Hills, 1982, p. 70). However, she adds a cautionary note that the socio-economic data Bristow uses to draw such conclusions is unreliable. In another article Hills (1983) suggests that life-style factors are likely to affect opportunities for participation and change during different periods in one's life. For example, with marriage and childbirth, domestic and family needs may mean it is difficult for women to get involved in local government. She discusses the role conflict theory and the concept of political efficacy which can be used to explain why women might not want to take up political office. The role conflict theory emphasises the traditional role of a woman and the guilt that she may feel if she does not conform to this, especially if it is expected that she do so by those around her. According to Hills, support of partners was seen as a factor in helping overcome this. She therefore highlights flexibility and family attitudes as being key factors in aiding women's recruitment. In respect of political efficacy, experience of employment outside the home was seen as promoting confidence and self-worth, whereas those working at home tended to rate themselves less successfully in their ability to debate and argue successfully.

A number of authors highlight theories around domestic and family circumstance issues. Martlew, Forrester and Buchanan (1985) highlight factors such as family support, flexibility and the availability of time as key factors affecting the likelihood of women getting involved in political activity. Full-time employment is also flagged up as a major barrier, although as noted elsewhere, this does provide experience outside the home and can therefore be seen as a useful factor in boosting confidence.

Galloway and Robertson (1991, p. 3) mention many of the reasons which are highlighted by other authors for the under-representation of women in party politics such as '...the timing and location of meetings... The lack of facilities, particularly crèche facilities and the cost of political involvement...', whilst Norris and Lovenduski (1995) also discuss the costs of political involvement and recognise that time as well as money and support are important resources for candidates to have. The financial costs act as a block on many women who have little money and few alternatives for child-care. In addition, finding the energy for political involvement is not easy when one has a family to look after. 'I'd love to change the world, but I have to cook the tea!' is how Galloway and Robertson (1991) highlight this problem using the title of one of the A Woman's Claim of Right (AWCR) conferences, arguing that 'These and others constitute very real hurdles for women in a way that they mostly do not for men...' (p. 3).

These issues are similar to some of those raised by Wilford, Miller, Bell and Donoghue (1993) who *inter-alia* cite family circumstances and responsibilities and link these in with what they term 'psychological factors' for example, lack of self-esteem. Barry (1991) also explores the barriers affecting women's involvement in local politics, citing domestic responsibilities, child care and lack of confidence, amongst others, with child care being seen as the most important. Women were also seen to '...have sacrificed their political lives or their jobs for their families and children' (p. 200) whereas men tended to sacrifice their families for their political careers. Barry notes the role of experience, particularly, '...the crucial role played by politically active mothers and other female relatives in councillors' lives – more than could have been anticipated from a reading of the literature on local politics' (p. 200). In addition, Barry describes the New Women's Movement as an 'unparalleled' '...motivator on the road to participation...' for women in local politics in London (p. 200). This reflects Brown's (1996) argument about a 'Third Wave of Feminism' in Scotland since 1987 (p. 41) raising the issue of better representation for women.

The issues highlighted above are very much linked in with women's access to and control over household resources (time, money, education, confidence). Schlozman et al. (1994) investigated the effect resources had on participation in the United States. They found that women generally have fewer resources to facilitate participation in political activity, but that if '...women were as well endowed with political resources as men, their overall levels of political activity would be closer to men's and their financial contributions would be considerably closer to men's' (p. 963). They also found that, in general, men and women followed the same paths to politics and confirmed the role of voluntary organisations in bringing women into political life. This reflects Bristow's (1980) findings in respect of the recruitment of women to the Conservative Party. Furthermore, Schlozman et al. (1994) found that overall, women have as much free time as men and that the availability of such time does not play an important role in the decision to stand for political office, although among activists it does affect the amount of time given to politics.

A number of authors consider women and political ambition. In the United States Carroll (1985) found that women were as ambitious as men at state legislative, county and local levels. She notes that '...low levels of political ambition may be one of the reasons why fewer women than men seek political office in the first place...' (p. 1242), but argues that once women have achieved office they are as ambitious as men. She concludes that to find explanations for the poor representation of women in senior positions it is necessary to look at '...possible patterns of discrimination and limitations in the structure of political opportunity...' (p. 1242). Here there is overlap with the structural explanations discussed elsewhere in this Chapter.

Costantini (1990) also considers gender differences in the motives of political activists in the USA. He notes that in some respects, the 'politics is a man's game' cliché can help to explain the under-representation of women in public office, but at the same time recognises that there are limitations with this. For example, the adage suggests that this is true at all times and places, however this cannot be the case since the numbers of women in the political arena are gradually increasing. Furthermore, it suggests that the nature of the game has remained the same. Although this may be true to a certain extent in that politics is often about power, conflict and ambition, it is quite possible to argue that the nature can change, as is discussed later in this Chapter about the ways in which men and women operate.

A further point raised by Hills (1983) is that *inter-alia* '...fear of discrimination may play a part in women's decisions not to stand for electoral office...' (p. 41). Whether or not political parties discriminate against women or not, if women believe that they do, then this may be a factor in preventing them from standing in the first place.

Structural Explanations

A variety of theories or explanations can be subsumed under this heading. These include voter attitudes, gender issues around women's role (for example, patriarchal attitudes and practices and male networks from which women might be excluded), organisation, structure and operation of councils, party influences (for example in terms of selection processes and procedures), political opportunity structure, the 'desirability thesis' and functional theories. In the same way that many 'individual' explanations link with problems of supply, so 'structural' or 'system' explanations frequently link with demand explanations.

Constraints imposed by the organisation and structure of the council have been examined by a number of authors, for example, Martlew et al. (1985) and Wilford et al. (1993). They raise issues such as the lack of consideration given to the scheduling of council business in order for it to coincide more readily with child care and family responsibilities and the fact that the formal structure of councils and the conflictual and sometimes aggressive mode of operation can be off-putting for women.

The role of party influences in recruitment is recognised by Bristow (1980) who sees these acting at two levels. At the more general level Bristow notes that the processes of recruitment and candidate selection (see also Barry, 1991) need further investigation in order to enquire into electoral discrimination but that '...the electoral system does not appear to act as a particularly discriminatory filter against women' (p. 85). More specifically, as discussed earlier, he considers the role of the different political parties in recruitment of candidates. The role and influence of party is underlined by Norris and Lovenduski (1995) who address issues such as the lack of women Members of Parliament and the social bias in the British political élite. Whilst their focus is on the national political system it is important for local government as many of the issues it explores are equally applicable to the local political scene. They discuss supply and demand explanations of gender on recruitment, suggesting that there is continuing discrimination against women and citing Austin Mitchell MP – 'The basic problem is that selectors are not enthusiastic about women candidates. They believe the electorate does not want them. They do not see women as having the same commitment as men... They fear that women might be unpredictable... in short they apply different standards' (Austin Mitchell, MP, cited in Norris and Lovenduski, 1995, p. 115). This reflects the earlier findings of Martlew et al. (1985) who undertook a survey of Scottish councillors in 1983 addressing issues such as ideology and attitudes. They argued that there is a masculine bias in the structure and operation of political organisations, which in turn impacts on recruitment.

Studlar and Welch (1992) consider the influence of the party system in elections to English metropolitan boroughs and found some support for the hypothesis '...that the more parties contesting elections, the greater likelihood that women will be candidates, and the greater the likelihood they will win' (Studlar and Welch, 1992, p. 64). In England, Scotland and Wales it is certainly the case that with the increase in the number of contests fought by the main political parties the proportion of women candidates increased and that a greater proportion of women councillors eventually elected (see Chapter 2).

Barry (1991) highlights 'The persistence of beliefs about women's place and male breadwinners...' and notes that '...delayed involvement in local politics... might lead to only partial assimilation into the gamut of party political values associated with local politics' (p. 200). The importance of gender issues around women's role is reinforced by Wilford et al. (1993) who refer to the differential treatment of women as a result of patriarchal attitudes and practices, for example treating women differently because of their sex or refusing to take them seriously in any role outside the home.

Mezey (1980) considers the effect of gender in the USA, citing party activity as the key to recruitment at local level. In this study the only major difference found between male and female representatives was '...the impetus they [women] received at home during their adult lives: their husbands were often involved in public or party office while the males' spouses were not' (p. 81). This suggests that having a supportive partner who is active in politics may act as an additional stimulus for some women to participate. This has links with role conflict theory (Hills, 1983) and Barry's (1991) point about the role played by other adults, and in particular female relatives, in acting as a motivator for women to participate in local politics.

From another perspective the Woman's Claim of Right Group also argue that another significant reason for the lower participation rate of women at national level is the hostile environment, noting '...concern at the level of aggression and "head-banging" which malestream [*sic*] parties accept as the routine basis for treating politicians in other parties, and, more significantly, in their own' (1991, p. 31).

Another dimension is the views of party selectors and voters towards women candidates. A survey conducted across the United States in 1994 for the National Women's Political Caucus (cited in Seltzer et al., 1997) found that '...two-thirds of voters believe that women have a tougher time getting elected to public office than men do' (p. 76). Following work in Cincinnati Brown et al. (1993) argued that 'Substantive gender based differences in evaluations of the office-related capabilities of male and female city council candidates were found. These differences may impede the election and political advancement of some female city council candidates' (p. 1). At least one-third (and in some cases a majority) of respondents felt that males and females were not equally capable of governing. Gender stereotypes were reflected in the views of this group, with women being seen as superior to men in areas associated with their traditional caring roles, such as child care, social services, and dealing with people, whilst men were seen to have leadership qualities and to be more decisive (also see Shaul, 1982). Female candidates are therefore at a disadvantage because voters see men as more able to meet the demands of serving on the city council. MacManus and Bullock (1989) have also highlighted attitudinal barriers to try to explain the paucity of women standing for political office in the USA, including sex-role stereotyping on the part of voters, party leaders and on the part of candidates themselves.

This perception is important because if it is to be believed then it may in turn affect the number of women elected to public office. Women may attract less of the resources necessary to run a campaign, fewer supporters and less media attention and as a consequence may find it harder to gain the backing of supportive organisations and individuals such as other politicians. Welch and Studlar (1988) undertook an analysis of data from the 1985 English non-metropolitan county council elections in order to consider explanations of the under-representation of women in local politics and found that the results compared well with their survey of local government candidates in the 1984 Scottish district elections (1987). They noted some evidence, although small, of discrimination by party selectors, particularly in the Labour Party. In addition the Labour Party appeared to be less receptive to female candidates in Scotland. This reflects the findings of Martlew et al. (1985) who undertook a survey of Scottish councillors in 1983 addressing issues such as ideology and attitudes. They argued that there is a masculine bias in the structure and operation of political organisations which also impact on recruitment. Further evidence for this was provided by research undertaken by the Scottish Local Government Information Unit and the Scottish Local Authorities Management Centre (SLGIU, 1995b). In this study one-third of women councillors indicated that they would have to make special child care arrangements in order to be able to conduct their council business, compared to one-tenth of male councillors. Hills (1983) also makes reference to the discrimination by political parties of women candidates as a factor affecting women's recruitment.

In their discussion of who gets selected and why, Norris and Lovenduski (1995) raise the issue of gatekeeper attitudes and state that some of those they interviewed '...were strongly convinced that party selectors were prejudiced against women applicants, or at least treated women differently' (pp. 127-8). However, they conclude that although critics often attribute the lack of women in Parliament to be a result of gatekeeper attitudes, their analysis finds little evidence to support this view and that it is necessary to take account of the supply-side arguments in order to seek further explanation for this social bias. Their finding of a lack of a support for demand explanations is interesting and provides a contrast to many of the perspectives discussed here. Brown et al. (1996) also note that such findings are out of line with findings from research undertaken by authors such as Vallance (1979), Rasmussen (1983) and Adonis (1990) all of whom see demand factors such as discrimination as playing a major role in the under-representation of women in politics. They believe that the explanation for this might lie in the fact that those interviewed as part of Norris and Lovenduski's research (1995) were those already involved in the selection process and 'In that sense the candidates are already a "successful" group of potential MPs in that they have overcome the many hurdles of selection' (Brown et al., 1996, p. 169). If this is the case one might expect those newly entering the selection process whether at local or national level to perceive that they have many barriers to overcome and that discrimination and gatekeeper attitudes are just a few of these.

In the United States the 'desirability thesis' has been formulated by some to explain women's representation at different tiers of government. This holds that '...the probability of women being elected to public office varies inversely with the power and prestige of those offices' (Engstrom et al., 1988, p. 38; see also Karnig and Walter, 1976). From this perspective women are most likely to be elected to positions which are the least sought after, of low status and which may be unpaid or poorly paid (Fox, 1974; Karnig and Walter, 1976). In the United States this thesis is frequently employed to explain why '...women are more likely to be members of city councils than mayors of cities (Welch and Karnig, 1979), and why the proportion of city council seats held by women is generally greater than the proportion of seats women hold in state legislatures or in Congress' (Engstrom et al., 1988, p. 38; see also Diamond, 1977; Welch, 1985; Sinkkonen, 1985; MacManus and Bullock, 1996). Amongst the hierarchy of elective offices in the United States, council seats are often perceived to be amongst the least desirable offices to hold, and, in the view of this thesis, therefore the sort of position to which women are most likely to be elected (Engstrom et al., 1988).

Men's experience frequently enables them to build up networks of contacts and information. Women entering into politics in general do not have this to fall back on (Shaul, 1982; Bledsoe and Herring, 1990). Also these networks can provide much information from which women are automatically excluded if they are not part of the network or invited to meetings or allowed to become members of particular groups or clubs. Lone women in politics may find it difficult to find a supportive group with which to identify (Shaul, 1982). They may find themselves isolated in a male dominated area. Male stereotyping of women is also a barrier for political participation. Shaul (1982) says '...it is difficult for men to see them as holding more than helping roles. In addition, men can sometimes behave protectively, which can prevent women from having the responsibility for more controversial positions and decisions' (p. 497).

In 1979 Welch and Karnig predicted that '...in the long run women might do better in district than at-large races because of the greater name recognition and financial support necessary even to get the nomination in at-large contests' (cited in MacManus and Bullock, 1989, p. 33). Work undertaken by MacManus and Bullock (1989) a decade later to see whether the earlier prediction had come true found that '...structural features are not significant determinants of female representation on city councils... Gender may still be somewhat of an impediment to representation – but electoral structures are not' (p. 46).

Seltzer et al. (1997) also found that the reason for the paucity of women in public office was that few women stand for public office. They suggest there is hope that encouraging women to run for office will actually increase the numbers who hold office, but point out that in the United States, there is evidence of a further difficulty facing women who wish to stand for office, as the political system is biased in favour of incumbents who have big advantages over challengers. They therefore conclude that further research is needed on the possible impact of changes such as reforms to campaign finances, term limits and multi-member districts in order to offset the advantages enjoyed by incumbents.

Is it true that women candidates are less likely to win than men? Seltzer et al. (1997) found that 'When women run, women win... as often as men do... Winning elections has nothing to do with the sex of the candidate and everything to do with incumbency' (p. 79; see also Zimmerman, 1992). They observed that people no longer voted for generic male or female candidates, but specific individuals with stated views, positions on issues, experience and so on. Thus the sex of the candidate was a factor but only one of many that entered into the equation.

In Britain the continual reorganisation of local government may also have an impact on the numbers of women entering local politics. Hills (1983) has argued that '...the reorganisation of local government has itself produced a cynicism as to the efficacy of the work involved, particularly, among those women who conceive of local government in terms of responsiveness to community needs...' (p. 49). A decade later Wilford et al. (1993) provided support for these findings, showing that some respondents in their study were deterred from entering the political arena by the lack of powers of local government; and that this was perceived to limit the chances of pursuing a worthwhile career in local politics. Thus some women may feel that the current political structure does not allow them to contribute enough, or that it does not value the sort of contributions women believe are important.

Other Explanations

Some writers, whilst recognising the importance of structural explanations, make links between political culture and representation. For example, Hill (1981) '...emphasises historical patterns and traditions which are likely to acculturate responses of the populace to female candidacies for legislative office' (p. 159) and notes that in general, although American politics tends to be male dominated, some variations in female representation across states does exist and that this indicates '...that some states' cultures foster female participation in politics while others do not' (p. 160). Hill cites Diamond (1977) in support of this explanation who suggests that Elzar's (1972) 'traditionalistic' and 'moralistic' political cultures may be applied to female representation in state legislatures and concludes that '...political culture provides a gratifying explanation of female representation. In spite of structural impediments, women can and will be elected to legislative seats in receptive cultural milieu' (p. 168).

Elzar (1972) applied political culture as an explanation of differences in representation to the United States. He recognised that political culture will vary by state and by community and developed two political culture types – 'traditionalistic' and 'moralistic' – to try and account for these variations. Diamond (1977) suggests ways in which Elzar's categorisation of 'traditionalistic' and 'moralistic' political cultures can be applied to female representation in state legislatures. She sees the former as discouraging female participation and being dominated by a male élite who seek to maintain the status quo. In contrast to this, 'moralistic' political cultures have been described by Diamond as potentially '...receptive to the values and style that have been associated with women – concern with the public welfare rather than personal enrichment and so forth' (Diamond, 1977, cited in Hill, 1981, p. 161). She concludes that such a culture may be a necessary condition for the recruitment and election of women legislators.

Approximately two decades later Brown (1994) also felt that Elzar's classification was useful in explaining the bias against females in the Cincinnati study (Brown et al., 1993), at the same time recognising the limitations inherent in generalising from one study to another. Despite this Brown (1994) argues that it is appropriate to generalise to theory and that it is possible to compare the bias against females in the Cincinnati sample with Elzar's classification of south-west Ohio as an individualistic-traditionalistic political culture. The traditionalistic element would mitigate against the election of women. A further issue raised by Brown (1994) is '...the degree of gender-stereo-typic bias present in any particular electorate' (p. 369). This is likely to vary across the board and will affect both male and female candidates.

Bledsoe and Herring (1990) note that 'The barriers women face in achieving anything approaching proportionate political representation are certainly more numerous, and probably more onerous, than previously recognised' (p. 221). They identify a number of political and perceptual barriers faced by women including strength of current political position and perceived political vulnerability. They suggest that women who perceive themselves to be weak in these areas are unlikely to try for higher office. In contrast they argue that such factors have little impact on the decisions of men to pursue higher political office. 'Men are more likely to be self-motivated – guided by political ambition... these other considerations largely do not matter'. Yet 'They are of great importance to women' (p. 221). Brown et al. (1996) referring to women's representation in Scotland, albeit at a national level, noted the importance for some women '...of being asked to consider themselves as candidates' (p. 171).

Elements of the political culture explanations and the perceptual and political approaches would appear to indicate that men and women are motivated differently in that they expect different outcomes from political office. For example, women are more concerned with public welfare as opposed to their own political ambition. Costantini (1990) highlights two areas of political life where women appear to have a significant role – issue clarification and organisational maintenance – arguing that women '...are more issue oriented and hold views on political issues that are likely to enrich the debate within and enlarge the ideological distance between the two parties' (p. 766). In addition, in respect of the organisational needs of the parties, Costantini notes that '...the women studied are substantially more committed to and involved in their party than their male counterparts' (p. 766). Costantini concludes that men and women appear to want different things from political involvement. Men tend to focus on the power aspect of political life whilst women are more concerned with and committed to principle and party organisation and maintenance.

An interesting issue is discussed by Hayes and McAllister (1996) in their consideration of the under-representation of women in Scotland. They raise the question that perhaps the under-representation of women in Scottish politics has been due to the fact that nationalism has long dominated the political agenda in Scotland and that equality of representation for women has therefore not had a high profile. One of the explanations they cite for this 'is that while the issue is salient at the élite level, it has yet to be fully articulated among the mass electorate. Voters are only gradually becoming aware of the issue...' (p. 154). They also suggest that the reason that the issue had only been addressed indirectly by two of the major parties in Scotland – the Conservatives and the SNP – was the emphasis of those parties on the constitutional debate, noting that 'Scottish political culture is likely to play a role in suppressing debate: since the late 1960s the constitutional question has been paramount, and has eclipsed all other issues...' (p 154). At the same time, however, it is also apparent that the processes and activities leading to the establishment of the Scottish Parliament created an environment where something much nearer to equality of representation is expected in that legislature.

Finally, it is clear that there are many and varied explanations for the under-representation of women in elected local politics. Some writers emphasise structural explanations and demand factors, whilst others stress individual explanations as being the most influential. An overall view would seem to have to conclude that their relative importance cannot at present be estimated, but that the factors which mitigate against a greater role for women continue to have a significant impact.

4 Selection, Election and Council Work

This Chapter considers the ‘career’ patterns of councillors from election through their period in office, including attention to the gender dimension and the impact of party. As discussed previously, the emphasis on the term ‘career’ is intended not so much in the sense of a job, but rather as a means of summarising councillors’ experiences throughout their period in office. However, there is some evidence from the surveys reported here that some councillors (and perhaps an increasing number) do consider their posts almost as jobs or careers and this is considered below and in Chapter 5. At the same time other respondents to the surveys did question whether ‘career’ was the most appropriate term to use. For example, one said ‘“Career”’ is perhaps not the word I would use – “you’re the only one to do it and if you don’t, it won’t get done” is more appropriate!’. Others commented ‘…more a vocation than a career – working seven days a week – up to 15 hours most days…’ and ‘I do not regard elected representation on a council as a career, as a career suggests forward progression which often isn’t the case in elected positions’. Chapter 5 examines further the appropriateness or otherwise of the term ‘career’ in the light of evidence from this and other research and sets it against the background of recent and likely future developments in elected local government.

Methodology

This Chapter draws upon a number of major sources of information: surveys of councillors in England and Wales and in Scotland, information drawn from the *Municipal Yearbook*, and data drawn from the collection of local election results in Scotland since 1974.

The Surveys

Two surveys of councillors were undertaken for this research. The first was a survey of councillors in Scotland undertaken during late 1995 and early 1996.

With the system of local government which had existed since 1974 due to cease from 1 April 1996 it was an appropriate time to assess councillors' 'careers' over the entire twenty-two year period. This had been a period uninterrupted by reorganisation and some of those surveyed had been councillors for the full period. One of the main initial reasons for undertaking this particular survey was to explore gender differences between councillors. However, as women made up less than one-quarter of all Scottish councillors the sample chosen was *all* women on the district, region and island councils, plus an equivalent random sample of men councillors from the same councils. Thus, for example, if Aberdeen District had 14 female councillors, 14 male councillors were also sampled from that District, whilst if Clydesdale had 5 female councillors, 5 male councillors were also sampled. In addition, because of the authors' growing interest in the notion of 'careers' and 'progression', questionnaires were also sent to all 'senior' post-holders (such as leaders and convenors) identified in the *Municipal Yearbook* who were not already in the sample, a total of 89.

Questionnaires were therefore sent to the Chief Executive of each authority for distribution to the named councillors. Four weeks later reminder letters and questionnaires were sent to non-respondents. Unfortunately the period coincided with much of the work preparing for the new councils which took office in 1996, and in particular with the setting of budgets, so that many potential respondents were heavily occupied with those duties. In particular this may explain the lower rate of return from Labour councillors who were more likely to be in power during this period. However, given these pressures the response rate was reasonable. Of the main sample of 666, 343 responded (52 per cent), of whom 179 (52 per cent) were female and 164 (48 per cent) were male. Three hundred and twenty-three people did not reply. In comparison, Martlew et al. (1985) had a response rate of 55 per cent for their 1983 Scottish study, Young and Rao (1994) achieved 67 per cent for a survey of councillors in England, Wales and Scotland in 1993 and the Scottish Local Government Information Unit (1995b) 60 per cent for their 1995 survey of Scottish councillors. In addition, of the 89 other 'senior' post-holders sampled (all of whom were male) 48 responded (54 per cent). In terms of representativeness of councillors in Scotland as a whole in party terms the position was (percentages):

	Respondents	Scotland
Conservative	15.0	14.6
Labour	35.2	42.7
Liberal Democrat	15.7	9.6
SNP	12.2	13.8
Other/Independent	21.8	19.3

A further survey was undertaken in England and Wales in late 1997 with a small amount of financial support from the Society of Town Clerk's Educational and Research Trust. With the greater variety of types of authority, in this instance sampling was based upon councils, with questionnaires being distributed to all councillors in an authority via the chief executive. The sample consisted of 3 county councils (13 per cent of respondents), 3 London boroughs (12 per cent), 4 metropolitan districts (16 per cent), 12 district councils (38 per cent), 3 unitary councils (10 per cent) and 3 Welsh unitary councils (11 per cent). In total 1474 councillors were surveyed with 618 replying, a response rate of 42 per cent. Whilst this was slightly disappointing in view of the results from Scotland, it nevertheless provides a significant picture of councillors in England and Wales. The variety of authorities in England and Wales makes it much harder to assess respondents' representativeness of other councillors, but a comparison with the Local Government Management Board survey (1997) suggests that in terms of gender and party there is a reasonable closeness of fit:

	LGMB survey	'Careers' survey
Female	27.3	24.6
Male	72.6	75.4
Conservative	20.5	15.5
Labour	46.4	50.8
Liberal Democrat	22.8	27.2
Plaid Cymru	0.5	0.5
Other/Independent	9.2	8.1

The data presented here for Scotland are unweighted: that is, no allowance has been made for the differential sampling of female and male councillors. This is primarily because the results vary only slightly if weighting is applied, and the unweighted results are intuitively easier to understand. The one area where weighting does result in a rather different picture is in the discussion of 'full-time' councillors, but this is covered in that section.

Similarly, the data from England and Wales are generally presented as a total. However, where analysis does produce significant differences between the types of authority these are included in the relevant discussion.

Other Evidence

In addition to the surveys, further analysis has been undertaken for Scotland on the career patterns of councillors. Scotland was chosen for this research for three main reasons: firstly, the timing with the demise of one system and the creation of another being an appropriate time to take stock of councillors; secondly, in Scotland information on council elections has been collected and collated since the 1974 reorganisation of local government (Bochel and Denver, 1974-1995), whereas in most of England and Wales this information has only been systematically collected since 1985 (Rallings and Thrasher, 1997a) (although Rallings and Thrasher (1993) have also published a summary of aggregate data for all local elections in Great Britain since 1973); and thirdly, the scale of the task, although still very substantial, was more manageable in Scotland, with its 453 regional council seats, 84 island council seats and 1158 district council seats.

This additional research has focused upon evidence related to 'careers' and 'progression' as councillors. For example, data from the *Municipal Yearbook* has been used to provide information on the chairing of council committees. This was done by examining the councillors identified as chairing each committee of each authority; although a number of the smaller Scottish councils have no committee structure (Badenoch and Strathspey) or have a very small number of committees (Stewartry). The *Municipal Yearbook* has also been used to identify the holders of 'senior' posts. This may be an imperfect method but it does provide a useful basis on which to start consideration of 'careers' following election to councils.

Data from the collection of local government election results in Scotland from 1974 has also been used in this part of the study. This provides accurate aggregate information on some basic matters such as the number of male and female candidates and councillors and party performance and also allows the analysis of the electoral success and failure of individual candidates.

Candidate Selection and Election

The selection of candidates is potentially of key importance in any examination of 'careers' or any consideration of gender differences in representative local government. Parry et al. (1992) when examining party campaigning, found that 'Whatever the gender differences may be at the higher levels of Britain's party organisations… there is, on the basis of our evidence, little or no gender difference in the recruitment of grass-roots volunteers to campaign for their favoured election candidate or political party' (p. 145). Yet when it comes to representation, whether in local or central government there are very significant gender inequalities.

In recent years candidate selection and election has become topical for a range of reasons. When Labour put forward women-only short-lists for parliamentary selection in 1993 it was seen by those supporting this measure as a way of positively discriminating in favour of women in order to boost their numbers. Despite this, the approach had to be abandoned following a successful legal challenge. However, the under-representation of women at both local and national level has continued to be recognised as an area of concern within the major parties. This has been illustrated by a proposal to the Liberal Democrats' 1997 conference, which despite fears of a similar legal challenge, aimed to ensure that half of all shortlisted candidates for the Westminster and European Parliaments were women; however this move was defeated. In addition, in Scotland the Scottish Constitutional Convention (1995) recommended that women and men should have equal numbers of seats in the Scottish Parliament. To this end following Labour's 1997 general election victory Donald Dewar, the Scottish Secretary, put forward a proposal to change the Sex Discrimination Act so that bias in favour of women candidates would not be open to legal challenge. This was backed by leading figures in the Labour Party such as David Blunkett, Education and Employment Secretary and Harriet Harman, Social Services Secretary, who feared that 'representation of women in the new Scottish Parliament or Welsh Assembly' might be low if no action were taken (*The Guardian*, 3 March 1998). Even when it became clear that this proposal faced a number of problems, Labour in Scotland effectively pushed ahead with its 'twinning plan': if a male candidate was selected in one constituency, a woman should to be selected in the neighbouring one. In addition the SNP also aimed to ensure a high level of representation of women. The strength of support for these parties effectively guaranteed that a significant proportion of the new MSPs would be women. By 1998 even the Conservative Party was rethinking the impact of its selection processes, with the Party Chairman, Archie Norman, attempting to encourage constituency associations to consider a wider range of possible candidates.

The discussion in Chapter 3 made clear that there is a reasonable body of literature that links the increase in women on elected bodies with the numbers of women standing for election. In Great Britain it is certainly the case that the greater the proportion of women candidates the greater the proportion of women councillors eventually elected.

Patterns of Electoral Competition, Success and Failure

In every set of local government elections in England, Scotland and Wales a smaller proportion of women candidates have been elected than men. For example, in the English shire districts Rallings and Thrasher (1997a) note that from the 1970s 'there has been a consistent gap of always less than 4 per cent between the percentages of women candidates and councillors at each set of elections' (p. 71), whilst in Scotland the gap has often exceeded 4 per cent (Bochel and Denver, 1992, 1994 and 1995). There are a number of potential explanations for this, many of which are discussed in Chapter 3. However, in addition there is one factor which arises primarily (although not entirely) from the outcome of each preceding election, and that is that women are less likely than men to have the advantage of personal or party incumbency.

Rallings and Thrasher (1997a) have examined the impact of incumbency in the English shire counties and found that in 1993 the three per cent gap in the share of the vote between all male and all female candidates narrowed to only one per cent when only male and female incumbent councillors were examined. However, there were party differences, with Labour non-incumbent women doing significantly less well than men, but Liberal Democrat women tending to outperform their male colleagues. When they examined the impact of gender in the metropolitan boroughs with their multi-member seats and the consequent party lists they concluded that men have traditionally enjoyed a more privileged position in the parties and have often occupied the safer seats, making male incumbents more likely to occupy first place in multi-member wards. Below first place on the list there appeared to be no impact from gender. Rallings and Thrasher (1997a) have also analysed voting in single-member wards at the 1990 and 1992 district elections in England and found that in both years male candidates polled two per cent higher than females. However, they argue that this is not due to voter discrimination, as the mean vote for male and female incumbents in 1992 was identical, rather other factors account for the discrepancy in share of the vote. In particular they suggest that the parties do not appear to select women for better seats.

Studlar and Welch (1987) consider the under-representation of women in local politics in Scotland. They conclude '...that women candidates are less likely to win election than are male candidates, and they poll somewhat fewer votes. These differences are almost entirely explained by the fact that women candidates are much less likely to enjoy personal or party incumbency, slightly more likely to run against incumbents, and less likely to be unopposed. Once these factors are controlled, women perform as well as men' (pp. 186-7). In other work (Welch and Studlar, 1988) they again cite incumbency as a major factor contributing to the under-representation of women.

On balance, there is little evidence that women candidates do perform less well than male candidates in British local elections, and compared with other factors the impact of incumbency is likely to be of relatively minor importance. However, this is a complex issue which may warrant further exploration elsewhere.

In Scotland it has been possible to analyse data collected by Bochel and Denver (various years) to examine the differential gender impact on each cohort elected to the regional councils from 1978 to 1994 (Table 4.1). Looking at each cohort of councillors (women in brackets) this shows that roughly one-third of seats on the regional councils were filled by first-time councillors at each election from 1978 to 1994.

The proportions of men and women councillors from each cohort serving the same number of terms was roughly similar with the exception of women from the 1974 cohort being significantly less likely to serve all six terms and the faster turnover of women from the 1978 cohort. There was little gender difference in the age of councillors, the mean for men being 52 and for women being 54, and the mean age when first elected was 45 for men and 46 for women. The percentage of each cohort being defeated at an election, rather than those who stood down for some other reason, is shown in Table 4.2.

Table 4.1 Number of terms served by each entry cohort, Scottish regional councils, 1974-1994 (women in brackets)

Year first elected	Percentage of cohort remaining after				
	Second election	Third election	Fourth election	Fifth election	Sixth election
1974	65.7 (66.0)	43.2 (36.5)	25.8 (18.3)	16.1 (6.9)	11.5 (2.4)
1978	66.0 (58.3)	37.9 (29.1)	22.9 (12.4)	14.4 (8.3)	
1982	61.6 (60.0)	36.0 (48.0)	26.2 (40.0)		
1986	71.9 (71.4)	48.5 (45.7)			
1990	57.6 (67.9)				

Table 4.2 Proportion of councillors defeated, Scottish regional councils, 1974-1994

Year first elected	Number of terms served (%)				
	1	2	3	4	5
1974	20.9	20.6	20.0	21.4	20.0
1978	25.0	32.5	26.0	23.0	
1982	38.0	26.1	31.2		
1986	19.1	23.0			
1990	42.1				

In addition, given the much more manageable scale of the task it is possible to undertake some additional analysis on gender at the regional level in Scotland – this is much more manageable than at the district level or for the various types of council in England which generally have much higher numbers of candidates and councillors.

The Scottish regions saw the same slow and consistent increase in the number and proportion of candidates who are women from 1974 (12 per cent) to 1994 (22 per cent) as did local government the rest of Britain, with a consequent increase in women councillors (from 10 per cent to 17 per cent). However, within this there were some differences. In 'non-partisan' regions (those where Independent candidates predominate) the proportion of candidates who were women increased only slightly, from 10 to 14 per cent, whilst in 'partisan' regions (where candidates from the four main political parties predominate) the increase was from 13 to 24 per cent; in itself unspectacular, but greater. Further, the non-partisan regions actually saw declines in the proportion of women candidates in three of the six elections, including the last one in 1994. In contrast the partisan regions saw a consistent, albeit modest, increase. One result of this has been that the partisan region with the lowest proportion of women, Strathclyde (19 per cent), was three per cent ahead of the non-partisan region with the highest proportion (Borders, 16 per cent).

There are a number of possible explanations for these including cultural differences, with the non-partisan regions being in some senses more 'conservative', the influence of parties, and in particular their desire to encourage more women to stand for political office, and differential levels of competitiveness which may both affect the desire of women to stand and the outcome of electoral contests.

The differences between partisan and non-partisan regions were also reflected in the proportion of women councillors. Whilst the number and proportion of regional women councillors rose slowly and consistently across Scotland, from 44 (10 per cent) to 79 (17 per cent), in non-partisan regions the increase was from 8 to 13 per cent and in partisan regions from 11 to 19 per cent.

Again, there may be a number of explanations for this, including that more women are now seeking election, the benign influence of parties discussed above, the decline of Independents, and the success of the Liberal Democrats and the SNP, both of which select significant proportions of women candidates.

Finally on this subject, rather paradoxically, whilst the number and proportion of women candidates and councillors is lower in non-partisan regions, the chances of women being elected are much higher there. In the partisan regions between 1974 and 1994 the proportion of women candidates elected fell by eleven per cent (from 32 to 21 per cent) the proportion elected in non-partisan regions rose by 14 per cent (from 30 to 44 per cent). This may have occurred for a number of reasons, such as the growth in the number of 'no-hope' parties, such as the Greens, in partisan regions, diminishing returns – with more women candidates it is inevitably more likely that they will be less likely to be elected, it may reflect the different electoral fortunes of the parties, there may be an element of self-selection by Independents, women might be more likely to oppose other women.

Women Versus Men Contests The analysis of this data is complex and time consuming. The analysis presented below (Figure 4.1) includes all contests that have taken place from 1978 through to 1994 in the Scottish regions only and can be summarised as follows. It examines the gender pattern in each contest – men only, women only, men versus women (where a man was the incumbent) and women versus men (where a woman was the incumbent). For all years (1978, 1982, 1986, 1990, 1994) the greatest number of contests took place among men only. Within this category, the largest number of contests took place in 1978 (294). The number of contests involving men only then declined in each election until 1990 and then rose slightly in 1994. The second largest category of contests was that involving men versus women. This started from a base of 83 contests in 1978, and apart from a slight dip in 1990, the number of contests of this type then increased each year. The third largest category of contests which took place was that involving women versus men. The numbers of these contests gradually increased over the period from 1978 to 1994, reflecting the slow increase in the number of women councillors. The smallest category of contests took place amongst women only. In contrast to the trends in the men versus women and women versus men categories and despite the increase in women candidates, the numbers of contests among women only declined over the period 1978 to 1994. Whilst the same analysis could not be applied to 1974 as there were no incumbent councillors it is worth noting that there were 309 contests between men only, 120 contests involving men and women, and only 3 involving only women, in each of which there was only one candidate.

Figure 4.1 Patterns of gender competition, Scottish regional council elections, 1978-1994

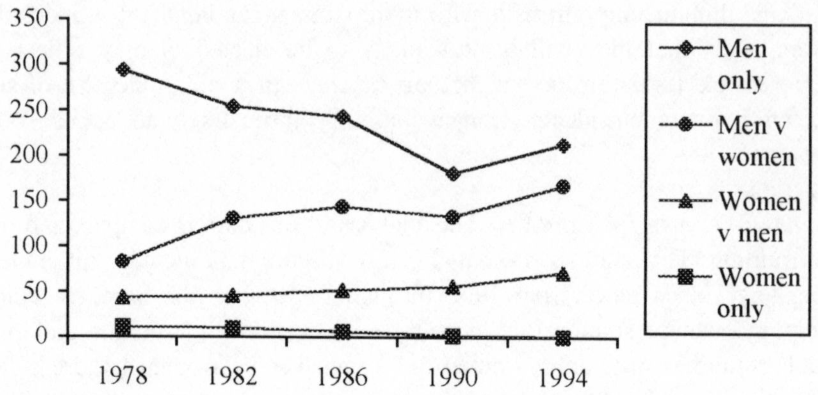

Council 'Careers'

Why Stand?

The main reasons cited by survey respondents for deciding to stand for election were generally similar in England and Wales and Scotland, although there were some differences in ordering. The most common causes given were a belief in public service (38 per cent of men and 45 per cent of women in England and Wales, 24 per cent to 33 per cent in Scotland), an interest in community and local issues (32 per cent of men and women in England and Wales, 25 per cent to 20 per cent in Scotland), personal satisfaction (28 to 35 per cent in England and Wales, 21 per cent to 23 per cent in Scotland), party reasons, such as being encouraged by the party or to help their party (23 per cent and 22 per cent in England and Wales and 31 per cent of women as opposed to 27 per cent of men in Scotland), and that the individuals were already involved in local politics, trades unions and/or community affairs (14 per cent to 15 per cent in England and Wales and 21 per cent to 9 per cent in Scotland).

With the increasing politicisation of local government and the dominance of party in many areas, at least some degree of 'formal' selection has become the norm. Over 95 per cent of Labour and Conservative councillors reported going through such a process whilst 88 per cent of

Liberal Democrats had done so. The vast majority of women and men candidates reported no difficulties in being selected as a candidate, whilst only six women (five Labour and one Liberal Democrat) reported some discrimination due to gender. Overall there is little evidence of discrimination in selection. Indeed more councillors reported difficulties with reselection (fourteen) and branch splits (eleven) although these still only represent a very small number of respondents.

However, whilst for some selection is the most important step towards election a significant proportion of councillors from the main parties had stood unsuccessfully before finally winning a council seat (Table 4.3).

Table 4.3 Percentage of councillors standing unsuccessfully before election

	England and Wales	Scotland
Conservative	15.6	22.5
Labour	34.7	17.8
Liberal Democrat	48.2	14.2
SNP	–	21.6

Council Progression

In looking at council 'careers' this section considers the number of senior posts held by women, committees chaired by women and the types of committees which they chair, with the data for this being drawn from Scotland where the smaller number of cases and the continuity of council structure make this a more straightforward and informative analysis.

For Britain as a whole, Young and Rao's (1994) survey of councillors suggested that women were as likely as men to hold senior posts such as leader, chair or committee chair. Our survey of England and Wales bears this out, with women being almost as likely as men to hold senior posts (7 per cent compared with 8 per cent) and very slightly more likely to chair committees, although the much smaller number of women means that senior post-holders are still much more likely to be male. Our research in

Scotland, based on analysis of selected returns to the *Municipal Yearbook*, rather than responses to a survey, illustrates how the pattern has changed since the 1970s.

The number of senior posts (such as convenor, vice-convenor and leader) on Scottish regional councils ranged from 21 in 1977 to 28 in 1992, falling to 25 in 1993. Before 1987 none of these posts was held by a woman, from 1987 to 1990 one post was held by a woman, and from 1991 to 1993 two posts were held by women. However, these were the same two posts held by the same two women.

At the district council level the number of senior posts varied from 92 in 1978 to 120 in 1992, with the number being held by women increasing from 6 (6 per cent) in 1977 to 22 (19 per cent) in 1993. In a number of authorities women held at least two of the senior positions at the same time.

Table 4.4 Scottish district council senior postholders, 1977-1993

Year	Total no. of senior posts	No. of senior posts held by women	% senior posts held by women	% councillors who were women	No. of senior posts held men
1977	95	6	6.3	12.9 (1974)	89
1978	92	9	9.8	14.1 (1977)	83
1979	97	9	9.3	14.1 (1977)	88
1980	96	8	8.3	14.1 (1977)	88
1981	98	8	8.2	14.3 (1980)	90
1982	98	8	8.2	14.3 (1980)	90
1983	98	7	7.1	14.3 (1980)	91
1984	98	7	7.1	14.3 (1980)	91
1985	97	12	12.4	17.1 (1984)	85
1986	97	13	13.4	17.1 (1984)	84
1987	98	11	11.2	17.1 (1984)	87
1988	98	11	11.2	17.1 (1984)	87
1989	97	13	13.4	19.6 (1988)	84
1990	113	16	14.1	19.6 (1988)	97
1991	118	16	13.5	19.6 (1988)	102
1992	120	17	14.1	19.6 (1988)	103
1993	117	22	18.8	21.5 (1992)	95

At district level women have a much greater share of 'senior' posts, although it is not easy to explain why. It is perhaps possible that participation is seen as, and in fact actually is more easily accessible at district level – closer to schools, families, jobs and so on – for women who have other demands on their time.

The results of the survey in Scotland showed that of those who held senior council posts 46 per cent reported that they were full-time. In England and Wales respondents who held senior posts were also more likely to be full-time councillors with no other employment. Perhaps unsurprisingly, senior post-holders tended to have more council experience, with their mean length of service being 14.2 years in Scotland compared with 8.5 years for councillors who did not hold senior posts at the time of the survey; in England and Wales the mean length of service was 9 years for senior post-holders and 7.3 years for other councillors.

Committee Chairs

Again, the smaller number of councils in Scotland makes it possible to undertake analysis of trends in the chairing of committees. Taking three years (1977, 1985 and 1993) from *The Municipal Yearbook* to give an overview, at regional level the total number of council committee chair posts has risen from 89 in 1977 to 104 in 1993. Over the same period the proportion of these posts held by women increased from 3 per cent to 17 per cent. At district level, again there has been an increase in the number of committee chair posts, rising from 329 in 1977 to 365 in 1993. The proportion of committee chairs held by women has also increased from 11 per cent to 17 per cent.

A comparison of the numbers and proportions of council chair posts held by women in regions and districts illustrates that the regions started out from a lower baseline in 1977 with 3 chairs (3 per cent) held by women, in comparison to 36 chairs (11 per cent) held by women in the districts. Although the proportions and numbers increase for both, in fact the proportions of women holding council chairs in the regions by 1993 was very slightly greater than in the districts.

Table 4.5 Committee chairs in Scottish regional and district councils, 1977-1993

Regional councils

Year	No. of chairs	No. of chairs held by women	% of chairs held by women	% of councillors who were women
1977	89	3	3.4	10.2
1985	93	9	9.7	17.3
1993	104	18	17.3	21.3

District councils

Year	No. of chairs	No. of chairs held by women	% of chairs held by women	% of councillors who were women
1977	329	36	10.9	12.9
1985	348	46	13.2	17.1
1993	365	61	16.7	21.5

Analysis of the types of committees chaired by women suggests that for the regional councils (Table 4.6) for both 1977 and 1985 there was an emphasis on what might be perceived as 'caring' roles – notably education and social work. By 1993 this appeared to have broadened to a much wider range, although education, social work and personnel remained significant, whilst the development of women's/equal opportunities committees in some councils had become apparent. Notably however, in that year there were no women chairing the often influential finance and/or general purposes committees.

For district councils (Table 4.7) there is a similar pattern for 1977, with environmental health, housing and leisure and recreation committees frequently being chaired by women, although a number were also chairing 'higher status' committees such as Finance and General Purposes. The pattern for 1985 was also similar, although the range was beginning to broaden with more women chairing housing-type committees and fewer chairing Finance and General Purposes. By 1993 the range was again much greater, although housing, leisure and equal opportunities figured significantly. In addition, there were also a number of women chairing committees such as Policy and Resources, Finance and General Purposes and Buildings.

Table 4.6 Committee chairs in Scottish regional councils, 1977-1993

Committee	1977	1985	1993
Police & Fire	1	0	0
Social Work	2	5	2
Education	0	3	2
Land & Buildings/Property Services	0	1	1
Appeals	0	0	1
Emergency	0	0	1
Women's/Equal Opportunities	0	0	4
Finance/General Purposes/Investment	0	3	0
Personnel	0	0	2
Rural Affairs	0	0	1
Transportation & Roads	0	0	1

Table 4.7 Committee chairs in Scottish district councils, 1977-1993

Committee	1977	1985	1993
Buildings	2	5	5
Environmental Health	9	7	4
Finance/General Purposes	9	2	5
Leisure & Entertainment	6	9	7
Housing	6	14	15
Manpower	1	2	2
Policy & Resources	2	3	7
Community Development	0	2	1
Women's/Equal Opportunities	0	1	5
Environmental	0	0	2
Other	1	1	8

Because virtually all councils create committees where they think they are needed and name them for their particular purposes it is difficult to combine committees under specific headings. It is therefore important to be aware of the make up of these categories. For example, the category of Environment Health is a general all embracing term for committees such as Environmental Health, Environmental Health and General Purposes and Environmental Health and Cleansing. Thus the categories could be composed of these singularly or in combination with the other named headings. Similarly the combined category of Finance/General Purposes in this case is made up of Finance, General Purposes and Finance and General Purposes committees.

Table 4.8 Committee chairs in English and Welsh councils, 1997

Type	Male	Female
Property/technical	4	2
Community development	1	2
Contracts/value for money	4	0
Economic	5	1
Planning/urban regeneration	12	1
Equality	0	1
Financial	5	1
Corporate	2	0
Policy/resources	10	1
Roads, transport	4	0
Environmental	7	3
Education	8	3
Public protection	3	0
Leisure/culture	13	3
Social services/policy	7	3
Housing	6	1
Personnel	4	4
Licensing	0	1
Environmental health/health	1	1
Other	0	1

Whilst such a thorough analysis was not possible for England and Wales our survey does provide some evidence of the type of committees chaired by men and women (Table 4.8).

Given the relatively small numbers, particularly of women, there are no clear conclusions to be drawn from this table. However, there is no evidence to suggest that women councillors are any more likely to be chairing committees associated with 'women's' or 'caring' issues.

Impact on Policy

The individuals who chair committees can be both influential and powerful. They have an important role in agenda setting and liaising with the chief officers of the council (Elcock, 1994). Similarly holders of senior council positions such as leaders, chairs and convenors, can hold powerful positions (Chandler, 1996). Leaders of the largest party groups, who may not hold a formal council title, also have potentially powerful roles, in some cases being the most influential member of the council. Given the power held by persons in these positions they are obviously in a key position to influence and impact upon policy.

Given that the numbers and proportions of elected women within local government are increasing, albeit slowly, along with the numbers holding senior posts and chairing committees, there is potential for women to make an impact on policy in a number of ways. Firstly, just by being in a position of power they are able to influence and impact upon policy; and secondly, there may be the potential to make a different impact from men in similar positions because they may operate in different ways. For example, research in the United States (Costantini, 1990) would appear to indicate that men and women are motivated differently, in that they expect different outcomes from political office, with for example, women being more concerned with public welfare as opposed to their own political ambition. Costantini (1990) has highlighted two areas of political life where women appear to have a significant role, described as 'issue clarification' and 'organisational maintenance', and suggests that women '...are more issue oriented and hold views on political issues that are likely to enrich the debate within and enlarge the ideological distance between the two parties' (1990, p. 766). In addition, in respect of the organisational needs of the parties, Costantini (1990, p. 766) notes that '...the women studied are substantially more committed to and involved in their party than their male counterparts'. Costantini concludes that men and women appear to want different things from political involvement – men tend to focus on the power aspect of political life whilst women are more concerned with and committed to principle and party organisation and maintenance.

This leads on to the related issue of whether women generally pursue different approaches to policy making, particularly in terms of a top-down or bottom-up attitude to policy-making. Whilst there is relatively little hard data, there is some literature from the United States which refers to women being concerned '...with the public welfare rather than personal enrichment...' (Diamond, 1977 cited in Hill, 1981, p. 161) and from the UK suggesting that women often organise at grass roots level often outside formal politics (Hersh, 1991) in a more informal, open and non-hierarchical way. This would appear to indicate that there is a preference among women for a bottom-up approach towards policy-making and problem solving. In addition, involvement in the local community can provide women with a good knowledge of local issues and useful experience in how to progress the concerns of the community, which can be important once in elected local government. If, as some have suggested, women do have a preference for more open ways of working outside formal politics then perhaps those who choose to move into this arena may be seen to transfer such an approach to the work of elected local government.

The way in which women operate and their commitment to achieving something worthwhile for the community as a whole, rather than just for themselves might also be linked to the types of issues with which they are involved. However, in our surveys the response to a question asking what issues they have been most involved produced relatively little gender difference. In order to explore what it is that women do once they become involved in these particular issues it may be that further and more qualitative research might be required. That said, in England and Wales women were more likely than men to be involved in equal opportunities (7 to 2 per cent) and housing (31 to 22 per cent). Men were rather more likely to be involved in economic or industrial issues (11 to 5 per cent), finance (21 to 9 per cent) and transport and roads (17 to 11 per cent). In Scotland women were more likely to be involved in the environment (22 to 15 per cent), equal opportunities (11 to 2 per cent) and housing (45 to 36 per cent). Men were rather more likely to be involved in arts and leisure (20 to 14 per cent), economic or industrial issues (17 to 11 per cent), finance (22 to 15 per cent) and planning (35 to 24 per cent). However, it is not possible to be certain whether these reflect the committees that each council member is on and the issues that have arisen as part of their membership of those committees rather than their original interest in that particular area.

Committee Membership

In our Scottish survey we asked councillors whether they had been able to express a preference for committee membership and the extent to which their preferences had been met. Just over half of the respondents (53 per cent) said that they had expressed a preference about which committees they wished to serve on and had been generally satisfied with the outcome. Two-fifths of respondents (21 per cent) had expressed preferences and had had some satisfaction with the outcome. Eight per cent had expressed no preference. Only four per cent were dissatisfied with the committees on which they served, all of these being because the party in control of the council had exercised total power in determining the membership of committees. With some of the smaller councils in existence at the time of our survey, in some instances all councillors were on all committees, or there were no committees in the councils.

Reflecting the analysis of committee chairs in Scottish district and regional councils discussed earlier in this Chapter, there were gender differences in committee membership, with significantly more women than men reporting membership of several types of committees, such as equal opportunities (17 per cent to 7 per cent), education (17 to 12 per cent), general purposes (20 to 11 per cent) and social work (14 to 11 per cent). More men than women reported membership of committees such as buildings/property (10 to 6 per cent), commercial/compulsory competitive tendering (10 to 5 per cent), planning/development/economic development (61 to 50 per cent), finance (17 to 13 per cent). However, whilst it may be appropriate to suggest that this reflects gender stereotyping it is important to recognise that on committees such as social work and education the gender differences are not great. In addition, given the evidence that many councillors were satisfied that they got their choices of committees they may have chosen these rather than being pushed into them.

Whilst the survey of England and Wales did not pursue this issue in such detail, 62 per cent of councillors had expressed a preference for membership of particular committees and were satisfied, whilst 15 per cent had expressed a preference and were partly satisfied. Only four per cent had expressed a preference for committee membership and were completely dissatisfied.

Constraints

Councillors mentioned a wide variety of 'constraints' on their ability to pursue council work. The most commonly mentioned were the difficulties of balancing employment and council work (32 per cent of councillors in England and Wales and 29 per cent in Scotland), balancing family and council work (20 and 29 per cent), lack of time (10 and 20 per cent), being in a minority group (10 and 14 per cent) and the restrictions on council finances (7 and 13 per cent). Women were more likely to identify family needs and being part of a minority party group whilst men were more likely to see the demands of employment as a problem and, in Scotland, restrictions on council finances.

The fact that women saw family needs as constraining their council careers is unsurprising and reflects the finding of much other research. Many of our respondents felt strongly about this both for themselves and for other women. Typical comments included those of one woman councillor who had decided not to stand again and said that she deeply regretted 'being forced to make this choice… the need for child care whilst undertaking council duties was in no way covered by allowances'; another stated that 'crèche facilities would greatly benefit women councillors (and staff) and encourage more women to stand for local government'.

It is worth noting that, in general, it appears that demands on individual councillors in terms of their workloads have become heavier. One stated 'I gave up part-time work which I had taken after early retirement, when I found my working day longer and more stressful than when I was in full-time employment'. Another said that 'a councillor is now expected to know more than before. The reading matter increases weekly. It is an impossible task with continuing changes of government policy and legislation'.

'Full-Time' Councillors

The remuneration or payment of councillors has long been an issue, and with greater politicisation and partisanship in local government, combined with increasing workloads on councillors the emergence of 'full-time' councillors is perhaps unsurprising. In our Scottish survey more than one-third (34 per cent) of the weighted sample reported that they considered themselves to be full-time councillors, although a number of these said that they were full-time councillors *in addition to* their normal occupation. Of those who said that they were full-time councillors seventy (60 per cent) had gone 'full-time' since 1990. This is likely to reflect a number of changes in recent years including the rising workload of councillors (Young and Rao, 1994; SLGIU, 1995), changes to the allowances paid to councillors (Hampton, 1991; SLGIU, 1990) and perhaps the spread of partisanship in Scottish local government (Bochel and Denver, 1974 to 1994). Of those who were full time councillors almost half had been full-time since they were first elected.

Forty per cent of women councillors were full time compared with 28 per cent of male councillors. This may reflect the fact that women were much less likely to be in full-time employment (29 per cent to 51 per cent of men). If this pattern remains, over time this might raise the prospect of increasing numbers of women rising to more senior council posts as not only will they increase as a proportion of councillors but they may also be those who are able to devote more of their time to council business and indeed to local politics.

Although it is rather hard to be entirely accurate at this stage, given the paucity of information available, there is a clear trend that councillors elected since the mid-1980s have been much more likely to become full-time either on, or soon after election. For example, 12 of the 22 councillors elected for the first time in 1994 were full-time immediately.

Of those who claimed to be full-time councillors, several had become such because of a change in their employment status, 11 (3 per cent) having become unemployed and 18 (5 per cent) having retired from work. Most of the remainder (20 per cent) had gone full time because of the workload and demands of council work, including 8 (2 per cent) who held senior council posts. Unsurprisingly, in the space at the end of the questionnaire left for 'other comments' thirty-six respondents, from all of the political parties, made reference to the lack of financial support and the workload in relation to being full-time councillors. None criticised the increasing trend to full-time councillors, although a small number did regret the rise of partisan politics in local government.

For the survey of England and Wales slightly more sophisticated questions were asked which resulted in 17 per cent of those who responded reporting themselves as full-time councillors without any other form of employment (a Local Government Management Board (1997) survey of councillors undertaken at roughly the same time showed 25 per cent claiming to be full-time). However, even here the picture remains complicated, with almost one-third of these people giving their employment status as 'retired'. Another approach is to examine income and here only six per cent of our sample reported council allowances as being their main source of income, although another seven per cent said that it was part of their main sources of income.

As in Scotland women were more likely to describe themselves as full-time councillors (22 per cent compared with 15 per cent of men) and women were three times as likely to have been full-time from first being elected (11 per cent to 4 per cent). Again it appears likely that there is a growing trend towards full-time councillors, particularly amongst those elected from the late 1980s, although the variety of types of council, dates of election and other variables make the picture rather less clear than in Scotland. There are also party differences, with 21 per cent of Labour councillors in England and Wales describing themselves as full-time councillors with no form of employment, compared with 13 per cent of both Conservatives and Liberal Democrats and 16 per cent of Independents. The reasons given for becoming full-time were similar to those from the Scottish study, with 30 (five per cent) citing retiral, 18 (3 per cent) unemployment, and 27 (4 per cent the demands of council work).

Politics and Political Ambitions

Almost all (95 per cent) councillors in England and Wales and four-fifths of respondents (81 per cent) from Scotland were members of political parties although forty of these had previously stood under different labels. Of those responding many held office for their party group, with 9 per cent in England and Wales (11 per cent in Scotland) being group leaders, and 6 per cent (21 per cent) deputy leaders. There was little gender difference in the holding of group posts, although men were more likely to be leaders and women to be deputy leaders or group secretaries. Respondents were clearly aware of the differential influence of different council posts, with 13 per cent of those from England and Wales saying that, given a free choice, they would most like to be a council leader whilst 36 per cent said that they would opt to chair a committee.

Many of the councillors had further political ambitions outside the local government arena, with one-third of respondents from England and Wales and half of those from Scotland expressing an interest in standing for election to another body. In Scotland there was little difference between women and men's desire to seek election to any of these bodies, but in England and Wales men were more likely to express ambitions to stand for another elected body, particularly a regional assembly or the European parliament. Table 4.9 illustrates those who said that they would like to stand for election to other bodies.

Table 4.9 Councillors' interest in standing for other elected bodies

	Women		Men	
	n	%	n	%
England and Wales				
regional assembly	34	22	159	34
Westminster Parliament	24	16	96	21
European Parliament	13	9	75	16
Scotland				
devolved Scottish Parliament?	68	38	65	40
independent Scottish Parliament	26	15	33	20
Westminster Parliament	26	15	22	13
European Parliament	12	7	18	11

Those who had been elected more recently, and particularly in the 1990s, were generally more likely to say that they would like to stand for another elected body. In Scotland however, of those who would like to stand for an 'independent Scottish parliament' more were elected in the 1980s, probably largely explained by the increase in the number of SNP councillors at the

1988 district elections. Among 'full-time' councillors, those who went full-time in the 1990s were also more likely to say that they would like to seek election for other bodies. There might be a number of possible reasons for this. For example, those elected more recently might be more 'career-minded' or politically ambitious; councillors' political ambitions may decline with age; or ambitions may decline as they experience the difficulties and limitations of politics and of power.

Expanding the analysis of the survey data on political ambitions shows that differences at the level of gender and party, both within and particularly across parties, vary significantly from England and Wales to Scotland. In England and Wales, for each of the three main parties, men were significantly more likely than women to acknowledge ambitions to stand for another elected body. In Scotland the only major gender difference was among Liberal Democrat respondents, where women were less likely to express further political ambitions. Whilst there is no obvious explanation of the differences between Scotland and England and Wales, changes such as the move towards unitary councils and the (at the time) likely imminence of a Scottish parliament might have served to focus the attention of some councillors on their political futures. Similarly, the debate over the possibilities of equal representation of men and women in a Scottish parliament might also have raised the hopes and wishes of women politicians there. Taken together these changes, and the apparently larger proportion of 'full-time' councillors in Scotland might have made the notion of a political 'career' seem even more apposite in Scotland than for many councillors in England and even in Wales.

5 Career, Vocation or Service?

Until the 1980s local government had two key characteristics which marked it out as autonomous: control over an independent source of taxation and the legitimacy conveyed through the electoral process. The changes under the Thatcher governments effectively removed the former and minimised the impact of the latter. In the late 1990s Labour's commitment to 'revitalising' local democracy recognised the difficulties in claiming popular legitimacy on very low turn-outs and the reality that in many areas local government appeared to lack relevance and immediacy to many electors, as well as the need to draw other parts of the policy making and implementation process into the realm of elected government.

Local government in Britain has been founded upon the same notion of representative democracy that has underpinned parliamentary elections to the House of Commons. One of the justifications for this has been that local government has provided the opportunity for wider sections of the population to become involved in political decision-making, although it is also true that consecutive reforms of local government from the 1970s have reduced both the number of authorities and the number of councillors. Nevertheless the notion of elected local representatives has remained at the heart of the operation of local government.

The traditional view of why people stand for local elected office and take on the role of councillors has arguably been that they have done so as a public service, but changes over the past three decades have not only changed the tasks which councillors are expected to undertake, but have to some extent altered the requirements, the workload and even the language with which we refer to councillors. Whilst it remains true that the use of the term 'career' may therefore still be stretching a point for many councillors, there are a number for whom it is perhaps increasingly apposite and many others who, whilst not necessarily recognising it or applying it to their own situation would be covered by a broad interpretation of the concept, at least for some period of their council membership. It is these developments and their impact that underpin much of the discussion in the remainder of this Chapter.

The Meaning of 'Career'

This Chapter, and indeed the entire book, is grounded loosely on the idea of local councillors' 'careers'. As outlined briefly in Chapter 4, this is based around the view that for many (although by no means all) councillors there is some sort of career progression from backbench councillor to duties such as chairing committees or to more senior posts such as party group or council leader. In central government there are frequent references to political careers and to the 'ministerial ladder', from parliamentary private secretary, to Minister of State, minister without Cabinet rank, and then a Cabinet post. Almost all ministers have to serve some sort of apprenticeship prior to appointment to the Cabinet and many have served for a long time in different junior positions. This type of progression is to a large extent equally applicable to local government with the potential to progress from a 'backbench' role to chairing a committee to political group or council leader.

In addition, our survey evidence suggests that an increasing number of councillors are, for a wide variety of reasons, devoting increasing amounts of time to council duties, and that in some authorities at least, many are effectively 'full-time' councillors. This makes further consideration of the concept of careers appropriate. Further, it has long been accepted that local government experience is one route to further political progress, including to selection as a parliamentary candidate, so that for a few councillors at least, local government may be the starting point for a full-blooded political career.

Herr (1990) examines the 'language' of career, pointing out that there are no right or wrong definitions or meanings, but that 'the study of career requires attention to the vocabulary of behaviour, processes, mediating variables, barriers, motivations, and contexts subsumed by the term career' (p. 3). From a psychological perspective he suggests that a career model is developmental, taking account not only of 'the sequence of positions one occupies over time, but the linkage between positions, the branching from one position to another, and the interrelationship of factors that cause persons to anticipate, plan for and implement one position rather than another at any particular point in time' (p. 5). Derr (1988) sees career as a long-term work history which is characterised by an intended and intentional sense of direction that allows for aspects of the individual's personal life.

What do we mean by career? Herr (1990) asks 'Is it different from occupation or job?... Are we concerned with who enters particular occupations and why, the individual differences in interests and abilities found in particular groupings, and the overlap in these characteristics across occupational grouping, or are we concerned with job satisfaction and work adjustment?' (p. 3). All of these questions are applicable to the work of a councillor. Many are covered to a greater or lesser extent in our research. In addition, as discussed elsewhere in this book, developments in the recent past and in the future are likely to make the concept of career increasingly applicable to local councillors.

The Gender Dimension

Where women are concerned many of the issues around 'careers' in 'normal' employment may be equally applicable to elected representatives, including those in local government. For example, Long and Kahn (1990) note that it is important to understand women's processes for coping with the way in which demands of family and work affect interpersonal relationships, career advancement and self-perception and that stress and coping strategies associated with these relate to job satisfaction, work performance, job tenure and overall psychological well-being. They also point out that 'Women employed in male-dominated careers experience particular problems stemming from gender-role stereotypes and occupational sex discrimination' (p. 235). This is nothing new to students of social policy (Hallett, 1996) or to those who have examined patterns of political participation (Parry, Moyser and Day, 1992) and recruitment (Wilford et al., 1993, Norris and Lovenduski, 1995). In the same way as women in male-dominated careers suffer from gender-role stereotypes and occupational sex discrimination the same may be true of women councillors.

Even when women in male-dominated jobs are successful and move to more senior positions they are in a minority and may suffer higher levels of stress than do men in similar positions (for example, Cooper and Davidson, 1982; Davidson and Cooper, 1984). Women may suffer from covert and overt prejudice and discrimination, isolation, lack of mentors, role models and supports, limited promotions and conflicting demands between career and family life (Hallett, 1996).

Whilst some writers have emphasised women's role in caring (Pascall, 1996) and occupational segregation (for example, Hakim, 1996; Walby, 1986), relatively little has been made of their contribution in what might be broadly termed 'public service'. This study takes some of this work a little further in relationship to women councillors.

Councillors' Careers

The literature on local government has from time-to-time discussed issues relevant to careers, although often in a tangential manner. However, Elcock (1986) characterised the careers of local politicians in three stages: the joining of a political party and becoming active in the party, serving on a local authority; and sometimes moving on to fight parliamentary seats. He also makes a number of other points which help to underpin the notion of progression and careers in elected local government: 'For most councillors who want to influence policy, committee work is the most important aspect of their work as councillors and their ultimate ambition is to become chairman or vice-chairman of the committees on which they serve' and 'The more able and enthusiastic members who are actively involved in policy issues tend to gain the positions of power, such as committee chairmanships or the leadership or deputy leadership of their party group and the council' (p. 72).

Chandler (1996) also made rather different links with the traditional view of a 'job' arguing that 'For many politicians, especially among working class Labour members, the responsibility of running a local authority presents an opportunity for job satisfaction that they could not dream of achieving in their ordinary working life' although he goes on to suggest that 'These members will be uninterested in radically new policies but wish to ensure the retention of conventional techniques of local government management and that serious authority wide problems… are dealt with effectively without creating too much censure from the local media. It can be suggested that the greatest number of local authorities are controlled by councillors of this persuasion' (p. 170). He makes the point that there have been what he terms 'professional councillors' for a considerable period of time and that 'The demands made on leaders of a city council are such that it would be difficult to undertake the task and, at the same time, seriously be involved with another profession. It is now possible for a leading councillor to secure a living wage although the resultant standard of life is not what would normally be expected from someone with responsibility for an organisation employing several thousand workers' (p. 173). Reflecting the discussion in Chapter 4, he also notes that many 'full-time' councillors are retired or rely on their spouses incomes.

Where language is concerned the term 'senior councillor' has long been used whilst more recently phrases like 'workload', 'job description' or 'job specification' have been applied.

In addition, councils have always been one recruiting ground for MPs and changes such as devolution, elected mayors, and the use of council executives or cabinets may make the notion of a 'career' yet more appropriate.

Remuneration

The issue of remuneration for councillors has periodically emerged as an topic for debate in the post-war period, and indeed has been considered by each of the three major surveys of councillors which have been initiated by central government: the first was for the Committee on the Management of Local Government (Maud, 1967); the second for the Committee of Inquiry into the System of Remuneration of Members of Local Authorities (Robinson, 1977); and the third was done for the Committee of Inquiry into the Conduct of Local Authority Business (Widdecombe, 1986a).

Hampton (1991) argues that these surveys suggested that the majority of councillors who were in full-time employment faced two problems. Firstly, they may have difficulty in obtaining permission from employers for absence from work for council business. Secondly they may suffer financially through loss of earnings while on these absences. These may also create difficulties or put off prospective councillors. Whilst many employers might be willing to allow opportunities for their employees to participate in public service, significant absences may be unacceptable or may disadvantage councillors in their career development in their area of employment.

In the immediate post-war years councillors were eligible for payments for loss of earnings or necessary expenses in the pursuit of 'approved duties', with the loss of earnings allowance generally approximating to the average male industrial wage. The 'approved duties' included council and committee meetings and other duties approved by councils in accordance with their functions. Following the reorganisations of local government in the early 1970s councillors were 'entitled to receive an attendance allowance as of right, without the need to demonstrate financial loss, for the performance of duties approved by his local authority' (Robinson, 1977, vol. 1, p. 15), with the maximum daily amount and the degree of discretion in defining approved duties being subject to central government advice or regulation. Co-opted committee members continued to be entitled to a financial loss allowance if they could demonstrate loss of earnings resulting from their council work (Hampton, 1991). The Robinson Committee was heavily critical of the attendance allowance system, arguing that it was widely misunderstood and that it did not take account of the range of a councillor's duties, left some better off than others, and did not adequately reflect the extra responsibility taken by senior councillors. It therefore recommended the abolition of the attendance allowance and its replacement by a combination of a basic payment, a financial loss allowance and a special responsibility payment for councillors occupying some senior positions (Robinson, 1977, Vol. 1, pp. 45-8). The government did not fully accept the Committee's recommendations but in 1980 the Local Government Planning and Land Act gave councillors in England and Wales the choice between loss of earnings allowance or attendance allowance, whilst giving local authorities discretionary powers to pay special responsibility allowances for councillors holding some positions, such as committee chairs.

In 1986 the Widdecombe Committee proposed the replacement of the attendance allowance and financial loss allowance with a basic flat rate allowance paid annually, with the retention of the special responsibility allowance (Widdecombe, 1986a). Whilst the government accepted some of the arguments the Local Government and Housing Act 1989 allowed the Secretary of State to authorise local authorities to establish schemes for the payment of councillors which could include a basic allowance for each councillor, an attendance allowance for specified duties and a special responsibility allowance for members who have such responsibilities. A separate scheme could provide for the payment of expenses and a loss of earnings allowance.

Another approach which has been mooted is the payment of a full-time salary to councillors. The Wheatley Commission (1969) favoured this approach but the Robinson Committee (1977) and the Widdecombe Committee (1986a) both rejected it. The objections to this system have been two-fold. Firstly it has been argued that if all councillors became full-time politicians this would limit the range of people coming forward for election and could alter the balance between them and council officers. Secondly, it could prove expensive if realistic salaries were to be paid and existing numbers of councillors retained. In countries where there are salaried councillors, such as the USA, there are generally fewer seats available. Yet it is undoubtedly the case that the demands placed on councillors can be considerable. Surveys have consistently shown the burden/hours of work of councillors; in particular senior positions can effectively constitute full-time jobs. By the early 1980s evidence was growing that 'There is a growing number of councillors, particularly in the larger cities, who have no other paid employment and who rely on allowances for their livelihood. The recompense is meagre, but when combined with ideological enthusiasm it helps sustain a new type of politician' (Hampton, 1991, p. 124).

Leach et al. (1994) point out that whilst it is rare for a councillor's job as a councillor to provide their main source of income 'there are ways in which material rewards (in cash or in kind) may act as a motivational force' (p. 175). For example, a system which includes attendance allowances provides incentives for councillors to attend meetings. They also identify status and power as factors which provide motivation for councillors. Where status is concerned they suggest that the more prominent a councillor becomes the greater the potential status rewards. For councillors for whom power or authority are key interests there are incentives to find a position (formal or informal) which enables influence to be exerted.

Leach et al. also argue that large increases in unemployment in particular periods have increased the number of councillors who are unemployed for whom attendance and other allowances provide a not insignificant source of income. Another economic factor which may be adding to the reality of the full-time councillor is the growing tendency for people to leave the labour market well before pension age, whether this be through early retirement, redundancy or ill health.

Councillors Views of Their Roles

Councillors have differed in their attitudes to their role, leading to the development of a variety of typologies. One of the most elemental divisions is that between those who concentrate on the representative function of being a councillor and those who prefer the managerial function of determining policy and ensuring its implementation. The Robinson (1977) and Widdecombe (1986a) reports both showed that whilst councillors spent about thirteen hours a month on electors' problems, the bulk of their time was used elsewhere. The research for the Maud Committee (1967) showed that whilst about a third of councillors preferred to deal with the problems of individuals, more preferred broader policy matters. Men and people in managerial or professional occupations preferred the policy-making aspects, whilst women and people in manual occupations preferred dealing with the problems of individuals.

Newton (1976), in a study of Birmingham, examined six dimensions of the councillor's role:

- attitudes towards the nature of representation;
- behaviour within council groups;
- preference for governing the city as a whole or looking after the interests of a ward;
- preference for dealing with general policy issues or with individual problems;
- preference for specialising in one area of council work or generalising across them all;
- attitudes towards the involvement of community organisations in the government of the city.

From these five dimensions Newton constructed five role types of councillors. The *parochial* he saw as concerned exclusively with individual problems in the ward they represented; *people's agents* extended this concern to a more generalised opposition to injustice and oppressive bureaucracy; *policy advocates* were concerned with running the city as a whole in line with policy preferences (for example as expressed in a party manifesto); *policy brokers* were less ideological than *policy advocates* and more likely to act as mediators and reconcilers of different interests; and the *policy spokesperson* spoke on behalf of their constituents on general policy matters, effectively being a generalised *parochial*.

In the early to mid-1980s some commentators identified the rise of a new urban left (for example, Gyford, 1985) from the left of the Labour Party which sought to encourage social change through using local government as a mobilising force for working-class organisations and radical action groups (Boddy and Fudge, 1984). Applying Newton's typology, the new urban left councillor displayed characteristics of both the *policy advocate* and the *policy spokesman*, with a strong commitment to a detailed election manifesto and to the decentralisation of policy decisions. In turn, Chandler (1996) contrasts ambitious, career councillors (but often framed in local terms) with parochial politicians, who are primarily concerned to serve the community and provide themselves with a worthy purpose.

From the point of view of the notion of councillors' careers the rise (albeit temporary) of the new urban left had some lasting implications. These included the more interventionist management style, the numbers who worked for local authorities (later outlawed by the Conservatives by the 1989 Local Government and Housing Act) and more particularly the number who were full-time councillors living off their allowances, and the challenge to the existing white male hegemony.

The greater emphasis on intervention and management led to a more interventionist style in much of local government. In addition, the professional experience of many of these councillors, particularly combined with frequent local government employment and the fact that a significant proportion lived full-time off their allowances were factors that arguably reinforced each other and created a further impetus for fulfilling the role full-time.

The attempts in some areas to challenge the white male dominance of local government also had an impact on councillors. Arguably there were three strands aiming at equal opportunities. One was the emphasis on services for black people and women provided by local government; a second was a stress on equal opportunities for people in the employment of local government; and a third was the encouragement of more black people and women to stand for election to local government. A number of developments reflected these changes including the establishment of race relations units and women's committees or similar structural changes and the emergence of more black people and women in senior council posts (by 1987 three London boroughs had black leaders), whilst more gained experience of council work and the running of committees.

Effectively looking at the starting point of councillors' political careers, Rao (1998) suggests that there are three key components to political recruitment. 'Motivations' include councillors' ambitions for public office and expectations of political life; 'resources' involve the time and ability to meet the demands of community representation; and 'opportunities' include membership or association with groups which select or sponsor candidates. Considering motivations, through examination of the limited British literature on political recruitment at local level Rao argues that 'the majority of local politicians are not motivated by any specific ambition but drift gradually into council candidature' (p. 293), that people become involved for a wide variety of reasons including ideological commitment and community service. On resources, he is clear that attributes such as socio-economic status and gender have a major impact upon the ability to stand for election as a councillor whilst being active in other community-related activities is another important influence. In terms of opportunities, membership of and support from political parties is an almost necessary precondition for election, other than in some rural areas, whilst Rao notes that some studies have shown that for Labour in particular, extensive party experience is important. In non-partisan systems, and in rural areas in particular, other 'community' organisations or informal networks often play a role in sponsoring candidates.

Case Studies of Councillors

In addition to the surveys reported in Chapter 4, the authors undertook a number of in-depth telephone interviews with councillors from England, Wales and Scotland in late 1998. These were designed to build upon the quantitative data gathered from the postal surveys and to provide qualitative information on three key areas: the reasons for standing for election, attitudes to council work and any political ambitions. The results of these are summarised as case studies below. They serve to illustrate a number of features of councillors' careers, such as the reasons for entering local electoral politics, the type of pressures on councillors, including balancing other work and caring responsibilities, as well as what for some may be a form of 'progression', and the nature of further political ambitions for a few. A considerable amount of space has been devoted to them as they illustrate clearly the feelings of a number of councillors about their experiences in local government.

Councillor A

Male, age 34
First elected: 1996
Labour councillor on a metropolitan borough council
Family circumstances: wife, two children of primary school age
Education: higher degree
Employment: self-employed

Councillor A had always been politically minded, a situation which he attributes to his upbringing. Before becoming a councillor he had been involved in community projects such as helping to set up a Credit Union. He owed much of his start in politics to a serving councillor who encouraged him and mentored him ('I had some really good grounding').

He feels strongly about the need for training for councillors in specific areas. 'Councillors are there to scrutinise the work of the council to make sure it is effective for the delivery of policies and the well being of the community. A lot of councillors aren't capable of scrutinising the policy developments of the officers. Very rarely do you find councillors searching for the problem areas in what has been proposed in the reports that officers put before them. Councillors do not have the training or skills to scrutinise what is put in front of them. The real policy makers are senior officers.'

In terms of policy, Councillor A has two main areas of interest: drugs and the development of community associations. The development of the latter is grounded in a belief in the need for people to take more control for themselves. He sees his approach as very different from the previous councillor who had been 'very effective in a paternalistic sort of way, reflecting the culture of the time'. Councillor A chose not to operate in the same way and argues that as a result the culture began to change ('It is easier for me to do this, times are changing, I can sow seeds and people can take more control for themselves. There are now nine Community Associations in the area and I have only been here two years doing this. Quite a lot of people don't even come back to me – they are busy running their own lives, so it frees a lot of time up for me to concentrate on policies, etc.').

He was immediately made redundant upon being elected to the council. He notes that two of the three councillors elected at the time that he was lost their jobs ('There are laws in the country saying you have got to give people time off work… but it is all garbage'. 'There is sexism and racism in the country, there are laws against these things, but there is no law against "councillorism"').

After being made redundant he then became long-term unemployed. In fact during this period he was offered two 'well paid' jobs, but both on the condition that he resign as a councillor. He refused and lived on family credit. He eventually began his own business and is now self-employed.

He once saw the council as full-time work – he never works less than sixty hours a week on both his council work and his own business (the time spent on council business ranges from twenty to forty hours per week and he adjusts the amount of time working in his business accordingly. He comments that the more time he spends on council business the more money he loses from his own business). Now he is trying to put in less time for the council, concentrating on putting in quality time. He admits that he used to put council before family – 'The problem is it is time demanding and if you are not careful your family will suffer. Mine did. I put importance in the wrong places. It is easy to do. I see others doing it and I wince.'

Councillor A serves on a range of committees such as Welfare Rights and Economic development and has recently been elected as a Deputy Cabinet Minister under the new council structure – 'short-cutting the expected ten year apprenticeship'.

He raises a number of concerns around the proposed council cabinets. Given that it will be up to councils to set the level of remuneration he believes that in general councils will not pay enough to attract people with the right qualities, so they will not be encouraged to give up well paid jobs to take on a council cabinet position ('We will end up with a 'grey guard' on the cabinet'). Secondly, he believes that there will have to be other safeguards 'it is not enough to say you have been democratically elected. There are all sorts of ways of getting favouritism built up to make sure you are elected'.

He has run in the past to be an MEP. He has ambitions for the future and sees standing for election as an MP as a possible option for when his family have grown up.

Councillor B

Female, age 50
First elected: 1990
Liberal Democrat councillor on a district council
Family circumstances: husband (also a councillor) and grown up family
Education: vocational/professional qualification
Employment: part-time employee in a small business

Councillor B initially got involved in politics through a local dispute over plans to build a supermarket on land that had been set aside for cemetery use – 'I felt very strongly about the issue and during that campaign somebody said it doesn't matter how much you protest outside the chamber at the end of the day the only thing that counts is a hand up in that chamber. I felt so strongly about it that I thought if I can't do it from the outside I will try and do it from the inside'. She stood as an Independent candidate and was elected. In 1997 she joined the Liberal Democrats.

'I think my main responsibility and duty is to the people who elected me. The main part of my job is to help them with any problems they have. That in some respects is the main reason I am there – they elected me to be their representative. I obviously do have a wider role. When you are elected you become a district councillor and are answerable to all the residents in the district, but I still regard my constituency hat as the most important one.'

Some of the main issues with which she has been involved include the refurbishment of an important civic building; building a new swimming facility; the development of an open space policy whereby developers have to provide on site play areas or put money into a local budget which is used to provide open spaces; the creation of a community park with woodland walks; and campaigning against the building of a supermarket on cemetery land.

Councillor B works three days a week in addition to being a councillor. She describes her council work as becoming 'fulfilling and very full-time [now that she is chair of one committee], because you are not just sitting there as a backbencher any more, you are leading the way by trying to formulate policy and you are pulled in different directions. The Department wants you to do more than your role of sitting in a committee, you become a figurehead and are expected to attend many other meetings. You are expected to be very knowledgeable as the chairman of a committee; you have to become an instant expert and know exactly what is going on'. In addition to being chair of one committee she serves on a range of other committees such as Planning and Policy and Resources.

She sees being a councillor as a combination of a career, job and a public service – 'It is all of them rolled into one'. Councillors on the district council consist of a good cross section of age and gender balance. In addition a lot of the major chairs are held by women. The council have helped to promote this process by introducing a 'carers allowance' which can be used for baby-sitters or for someone to look after anybody elderly or infirm. 'So, there is support there for women who are often left in the carers role, so that's why I think we tend to attract more women'.

Her ambition is to continue to fulfil her role as a councillor.

Councillor C

Male, age 57
First elected: 1994
Liberal Democrat leader of a district council
Family circumstances: wife
Education: diploma and vocational/professional qualification
Employment: retired

Councillor C had always had an interest in local affairs and politics. He previously worked for an MP. His wife was a councillor. He then retired early and was elected as district councillor. He also has experience as a county councillor.

He describes the main aspects of his position as 'the job of running the council, dealing with the policy decisions, working with the officers, working very much with the chief executive of the council, being available always because one is there as their employer. I represent the employer – councillors are the employers as far as councils are concerned. The officers are there to carry out work according to our policy, so one has to be there all the time to provide that political direction as to what is going on. So there is that aspect of it which is quite important, but very importantly it is the aspect which I quite like'. He finds dealing with the political group hard – 'you are dealing with lots of very strong minded people and they are all activists, they have all got their own particular thing why they are there, they are very concerned about their own areas. My job is to try and get a corporate view from them and that isn't always easy'. In addition there is a significant element of constituency work. 'The other aspect of the work, of course which is very important is the public relations side of it… there is a need all the time to keep stuff flowing into the paper to try and provide a positive image for the council as a whole'.

The main issues that Councillor C has been involved in include budgets and the Direct Labour Organisation. He reflects on his county council experience: 'Being chairman of the county council finance committee was quite challenging, particularly when each year your budget is £10 million less. The county council budget went down by £70 million in four years. It was very stressful to manage. We had to make decisions whether we maintained our roads or kept teachers in front of children in the schools. It got down to that level'.

Councillor C spends 50-60 hours a week on council business. 'I get up in the morning, there is a load of post to pick up immediately, I am on the telephone to my secretary at 8.30 am before I even leave the house and I usually have my first meeting at 10 am somewhere. I will usually have at least one meeting during the morning, maybe two meetings in the afternoon and I will have a meeting every evening'. 'As far as I am concerned it is a full-time job, it is more than a full-time job, being leader of a district council and trying to combine that with other public duties as well'. 'You can't do the leader's job on the council unless you are able to spare the time to do it full-time'.

'Having reached the position of leader it is probably one of the most challenging jobs I have ever had in my life. Some people thrive on it, go on election after election. As far as I am concerned I am quite willing to do it for a limited period of time… The telephone is always going at home and at the office, my life has ceased to become my own'.

He has no ambitions to take his political career any further. 'It depends on the age you get into this business. There is no way I would want to be living in London during the week and coming back here at weekends, although I do think sometimes that being a member of Parliament is a jolly sight less stressful than being a leader of a council'.

Councillor D

Male, age 43
First elected: 1995
Labour councillor on a district council
Family circumstances: partner and one child of primary school age
Education: degree
Employment: self-employed

Councillor D was involved in voluntary work before becoming a councillor. He joined the Labour Party and at the suggestion of the party stood for election – 'The party needed to field a candidate against a sitting Tory councillor of 19 years, it was more a case of fielding a candidate rather than having a serious thought of getting elected'. He was elected.

He sees councillors as belonging to one of two groups: firstly, the constituents' councillor who takes up and deals with personal issues of constituents, and secondly what he describes as politically aware councillors, who are more interested in policy and looking at their own political beliefs and seeing how they can shape policies to achieve those beliefs. He sees himself as belonging to the second group – 'Not all councillors are politicians, a lot of them are members of a political party because of social reasons, not necessarily political beliefs… They will come into the political arena without necessarily fully understanding party politics – they will vote Labour, because they have always voted Labour – there was not any other way'. 'Some councillors – often of the constituency variety – will be led by others on council especially if they are unsure about a particular policy. They may therefore tend to take their lead from someone else – if A thinks the policy is good enough, then it is okay for me. Thus they vote on an issue without really having thought about it'.

The main issue with which he has been involved is housing. Councillor D spends between ten and thirty hours a week on council business, but notes that it can vary considerably and sometimes spends twelve or thirteen hour days on council activity, although this is unusual. He does not describe council work as a full-time position – 'I think it would be better for the community if it was. It can be even now, but because it isn't paid there are lots of people who can't afford to let it be. I would like to [be full-time] but I have to earn a living to pay the mortgage, etc., so my time is restricted'. He believes this is the same for many councillors.

He feels that society would be much better off if councillors were able to devote their skills full-time to council work and gives the example of two female councillors in their twenties, on his council, who work – 'Both are very in tune politically. There are times when their jobs dictate that they can't get back for a meeting, so the council does not get their input and is worse off for this'. He feels there is a need for councillors to be full-time, but says that if this was to happen it would be necessary for the position to have full-time pay.

Councillor D is self-employed and works on a range of different things from bricklaying and decorating to legal work. In addition he has a small number of flats which he rents out.

He views his role on the council as 'more on the lines of public service, there is no career to it because even if you are in a safe seat I always associate a successful career with to a certain extent having a successful bank balance'. 'There is no money in local government… it is a temporary career, it is good for the community, but I think you need to believe in the politics that you are trying to push forward. There isn't really any other payback than seeing that things that you are doing are helping society… As regards career, there is none'.

Councillor D is vice-chair of one committee and an ordinary member on a range of others such as Policy and Resources. In the past he has held positions in the party, such as Branch Chair and editor for the Branch Newsletter, but relinquished these once he was elected.

His future ambitions are possibly to become a county councillor. However, given that 'the county council meets during the day and because they are daytime meetings you have to allow the whole of the day. I just couldn't give it the time'. Or he would like to become an MEP – 'I would prefer Europe to Westminster. I see that as the future for the world'.

Councillor E

Male, age 49
First elected: 1992
Liberal Democrat councillor on a district council
Family circumstances: wife
Education: no formal educational qualifications
Employment: self-employed

Councillor E had no previous experience of being involved in local/community issues '...but I have got very strong views on many things'. 'I was actually approached by the Liberal Democrats... they needed to find another candidate to fight the election when it was called'.

Councillor E felt that dealing with his constituents queries was one of his priorities but that analysis of government policy was also important. 'We are all human beings, the people who draw up these white papers don't necessarily get everything right. It is therefore very important that there is discussion of white papers, etc.'.

The main issue with which councillor E has been involved is planning. He gives the example of plans put forward by one of the supermarket giants to build a supermarket in the town. This created a lot of upset amongst local people and there were demonstrations outside the council offices. Councillor E was in favour of this development because he felt it was a bit more upmarket than some of the other supermarkets and might pull people in from the wider surrounding area. 'Now this is what we are expected to do, is bring life back into the high street, because the outgoing government screwed it all up by encouraging retail parks that took people out of the town.'

Councillor E describes his attitude to council work as a 'hands on approach'. When somebody telephones him he tries to go round and see them face to face. He will talk to all the relevant people and follows individual cases through. This he believes puts him in a much better position to argue his constituents' cases.

The amount of time he spends on council business varies, but he aims to go to all meetings. Alongside this he runs his own business. He estimates that approximately one or two per cent of his income comes from council work – 'Being a councillor isn't a full-time job. But if it was possible to do it as a full time job, I would seriously consider putting myself forward because I feel strongly about a lot of things that are going on. I wouldn't necessarily worry too much about what the wage was because I tend to get stuck in and I enjoy doing it'. 'I would like to see it as a [full-time] job because I could then devote all my time to it. It is definitely a public service and many people seem to think that it is a well paid full-time job but it isn't. You get your allowances but you would never live or get fat on those. It is good in so far as you then do it because you feel strongly enough that you want to protect and safeguard the environment that you live in and the people that live around you in it'.

Councillor E has previously chaired a committee and is currently on a range of committees including Planning.

He is considering putting himself forward as a possible candidate for his local parliamentary constituency.

Councillor F

Male, age 45
First elected: 1988
Labour councillor on a Scottish unitary council
Family circumstances: wife, grown up children
Education: Highers (then took degree during time as councillor)
Employment: full-time employee

'Originally I got into politics through the Trade Union movement and I joined the Labour Party. I had worked for a number of people standing for election in the past and I just became interested in it. A few people suggested that I put my name forward so I considered it and decided to give it a try.'

He views the priorities of council work as 'Initially dealing with constituents, that's what you are elected for and then following through from your dealings with them you get a better view of what's needed within the city'. However there is a need to strike a balance between dealing with constituents and formulating and implementing policy. The main issue with which he has been involved over his council career is that of budgets.

Councillor F points out that 'The hours worked [as a councillor] vary according to the role you are undertaking. At the moment I am working on average twenty to thirty hours a week', but that he is effectively 'on call 24 hours a day, seven days a week'. He described his previous role as Deputy Leader and Finance Convenor as 'full time'. With the hindsight of his time as Deputy Leader and his current position as an 'ordinary' councillor he now believes that 'there is a need for some councillors to be full time'. He explains this by saying that 'you need to retain the voluntary element because it is essential to keep in contact with the community outwith the council. It is very difficult to strike a balance because if you take on a post such as a convenorship it is a full-time job, but if you are a councillor with no specific post then you can cope with it as a part-time job… So I do see a need for not necessarily an executive of councillors, but certainly a body of councillors that are full-time and can look much deeper into the running of the council – planning strategies that type of thing – because you can get bogged down. At the moment a lot of reports that are coming to committees maybe do not need to be there. That's why councillors really need to look at the workload and reorganise. The city council is currently doing that'.

In addition to undertaking council duties Councillor F works as a full-time researcher for an MP. After 11 years, he has decided not to stand again and stood down in May 1999. He says, 'I have made a contribution to the city for 11 years and now it is time to consider myself and my family'.

Councillor F views his council work not as a career, but more of a public service. He also raises the issue of work circumstances. He says, 'When I first started work I was employed by a public corporation which was supportive of my taking time off for council duties'. At this time he was a district councillor and his work colleagues and his employer were helpful and supportive. He does recognise that 'Things change a bit though once you move into what you have now, which is an authority that covers all the spectrums – that is taking on the role of what was a regional council taking on social work, education, etc. – this has made it a much bigger role and increased the time commitment'.

Councillor F was Deputy Leader for around three years and was on a range of committees (such as Finance, Personnel and Arts and Recreation), sub-committees and working parties.

After being a serving councillor since 1988 he is 'Taking time out to concentrate on my working career rather than any political career at the moment. But what I do intend to do is to get back into being involved in the Trade Union movement, going back to my roots if you like'.

Councillor G

Female, over 60
First elected: 1984
Liberal Democrat councillor on a Scottish unitary council
Family circumstances: widowed, grown up family
Education: higher degree
Employment: Minister of the Church

Councillor G has been a Minister since 1955. She came across many social problems in her ministry and community work such as redundancy, unemployment, poverty, poor housing and run down estates. She found that 'much needed doing in the community but that it was difficult to get things done'. She saw a need for a councillor to take on this role and was asked to stand by people who were working with her and by people from a number of political parties.

She sees her role as a councillor as dealing with both constituents and policy and views both as important elements. 'I often find that dealing with constituents is very pastoral in many ways. I have a different way for constituents than for church members. I respect them and that's how we meet. I have surgeries for complaints and difficulties that constituents bring up and I live in my area so I know quite a lot of them. I think it's very useful if they come and confirm what one sees and what one hears and we work together to solve the problems. I will work with groups of people to solve the problem whatever it is and whoever they are'. 'The next stage – bringing things to committee or bringing them before the council. I am trying to get things improved, that's important. The group helps and we discuss and then put up policy motions in the different committees. If something is not working you can ask questions or you can again discuss it with other councillors and officials'.

Councillor G notes that there is 'an ever-increasing workload'. 'The council itself has committees and one tries to do one's best on these committees and that takes quite a lot of time. So do the sub-committees and reading the papers and doing a bit of research'. She discusses responding to Parliamentary papers, being involved in undertaking surveys on specific issues such as the environment in the local area, in order to feedback information to MPs and then responding to the feedback from them. 'I have very few nights off. Keeping abreast of the times – new equipment, the web, reading etc., so I am busier than ever. I have every sympathy for new councillors coming in who will come into this surge forward of IT providing so much information and always updating it. Councillors may well become full-time employees'.

The main issues with which she has been involved include poor housing and hospital closures.

Councillor G works full-time as a Minister of the Church; she therefore combines her council work with this. She believes that being a councillor could well become a full-time job, 'Though there is something about being paid your expenses, not being out of pocket, but when one is constantly giving in some way and the energy and time you do spend, and paying for domestic help, window cleaning, etc., there comes a limit to not being full-time and therefore receiving a proper salary'. Yet despite this she says that 'I see the work of a councillor as a public service. To me it has been an extension of my Ministry and my congregation. I've always asked permission to stand and they have always stood behind me and said 'of course, this is great, you must'. I think it has been an extension of my ministry because people know they can come to me in confidence… That has been something I've felt very pleased about and I've been able to have an input on matters that really affect people in the neighbourhood and in the whole of the area really. I've also kept up my voluntary work in the Community Association and yearly local festival, and many other committees and fought to keep our hospitals open, not very successfully but strangely enough they are both going to be opened and used for a variety of functions such as, children's provision, residential care for older people, flats and ordinary housing.'

'I do think that there is an expertise needed and therefore in some ways for many people it has to be a career and that maybe what has to happen in the future. I know that I have some colleagues, who like myself hope that you can, as it were do both – that depends very much on what is going to happen after the [Scottish] Parliament comes in – because that will make a big change and I hope for the better, I hope there will be far more co-ordination between Parliament and councils on how they will work at suitable, sensible hours… I just know my days are full with what I have got and I can do this because I have a very small congregation and they are right behind me. I have had a tremendous amount of support from local people whatever party they belong to'.

Councillor G is currently spokesperson on Housing and Personnel Management and serves as an ordinary member on a number of other committees such as Social Work and Economic development. She is also the Vice-Chair of the Constituency Party.

Looking to the future, she says 'I would like to continue my work as a councillor'. She stood again in 1999 despite boundary changes because 'These are exciting times and they need older heads as well as younger heads. They need the experience of the mature and the exuberance of the young to give to each other to move forward to this wonderful new era of great promise'.

'I would have loved the [Scottish] Parliament to have come sooner and to have stood for it'. 'I was chosen to stand as a prospective candidate but my husband took a heart attack and I had to withdraw'.

Councillor H

Female, age 46
First elected: 1988
Labour councillor on a Scottish unitary council
Family circumstances: husband, two children of school age
Education: degree and vocational qualification
Employment: self-employed

Councillor H had previous experience of working on community issues. For example she had been involved in a local campaign to stop a nursery being closed and found that getting involved in one thing led to another. Her direct involvement in politics came about because she was 'angry at the dismantling of things under Thatcher that it had taken her family generations to build up'. She therefore started to attend ward meetings and someone suggested she put her name forward when they were making up names for the panel. She was selected as the candidate and stood. 'It was the safest Tory seat in the Town'. She wasn't expected to win, 'just to make an effort so the defeat wasn't too embarrassing. I won. I was doing part-time teaching at the time and just wasn't prepared for being elected. I didn't even know where the Chambers were'.

She believes all aspects of council work to be important. Her main area of interest is environmental issues – 'For me personally I have fought long and hard on environmental issues and I have I feel made a significant difference, in that at first people used to laugh. They used to seriously laugh at me. They didn't even bother to be polite. In terms of environmental things they used to say "Look you are middle class. These are middle class issues", but I've been validated if you like, by the moods of national government and by many of the new laws that have come through. If we hadn't moved the way I'd pushed them to move, we would be in a much more uncomfortable situation'.

Councillor H says that her council work is at least a forty hour week commitment. She makes the comment that when she was first elected she remembered feeling that 'she belonged to everybody and at anytime of the night or day' and said that it was '…enormously difficult to ring fence any of your time for yourself'.

Councillor H is uncertain about council work as a full-time position because 'in order to be able to define it you have to be able to link it up to comparable jobs and I don't know one comparable job. If you have someone who is unwilling and lazy they could turn it into quite a small part-time job, whereas if you have someone who is quite dedicated it will be more than a full-time job and yet they could be performing the same functions. It very much depends on the individual'. In addition to her council work she works as an aromatherapist, a job that she describes as 'a paying hobby'.

Councillor H raises issues around the time commitment involved in being a councillor and the level of remuneration – 'It takes up so much time that I was relieved when the remuneration for it became a reasonable substitute for a job. To attempt to do it and a job means you have to sacrifice far too much of your home life, but at the same time it is very, very different from a job and there are elements of it that you hope are purely public service. I think the public also are confused and it means that in some way they respect you because they know that you have given up a lot to be a councillor and in another way they despise you because they think you are junketing on the rates'.

'When I started the remuneration was appalling and in order to do it with two young children I had to stop doing the part-time teaching I was doing because I couldn't juggle it all, but as they grew older I was able to do a bit more part-time teaching and manage to balance the books a little better. At the same time the remuneration was increasing anyway. When the government set up the new unitary authorities in Scotland they effectively made me unemployed because I could not work for the same local authority I was a councillor for'. Furthermore, an additional aspect of changes to local government legislation under the Conservatives is that she cannot work for the authority for which she is currently a councillor for a year after she leaves the council.

She is currently a convenor of one committee, but because of the approach to committees of the authority attends all committees apart from working groups and sub-committees. She also chairs a national committee (COSLA service forum). In the past she has held posts such as Ward Treasurer and fund raiser.

She put herself forward for the Scottish Parliament but got knocked out in the interview stage. 'I am at a real cross-roads just now. I have no idea what I should do. I've never viewed myself as a politician, just somebody who accidentally fell into it, but I get so irritated by the people I see who stand up and start speaking for the Labour Party, that it spurs me to get involved, but it's not the same political ambition that I've seen in others, where it's part of their identity, they feel they are politicians.'

Councillor I

Female, age 42
First elected: 1984
Labour councillor on a Scottish unitary council
Family circumstances: husband, school age children
Education: degree and vocational qualification
Employment: full-time councillor

Councillor I was involved in various community activities such as the school under-5's centre and also in a campaign to prevent the closure of one of the primary schools prior to standing for the council. She gained political experience by standing for an unwinnable seat 'So I had stood two years previous to being elected'.

The main issues she has been involved in include housing, education, economic development the location of jobs and the regeneration of areas of deprivation.

Councillor I believes it is difficult to separate out which elements of the job are the most important 'because you are there to represent your constituents, but you are not going to make a difference to them unless you can actually change policy and be strategic in some ways as well. It is a dual role'.

She is involved with many groups including an organisation to promote community dance and a range of bodies in the field of urban regeneration. She chairs a strategic body for urban renewal and sees this as a pressure group because it is a way of bringing decision-makers together in order to regenerate the whole area.

In terms of time spent on council business she says 'I am a full-time councillor, but I have children as well, so it is quite difficult to assess the number of hours I work. Sometimes you can be out every night and other times you are not, and sometimes you have weekends and sometimes you don't. I am mostly in from about 9 to 4 and then you have got things at night five days a week. The answer is five days a week mostly and then you are going out at least three evenings as well'. She views her council role as a mixture of career, job and public service.

Councillor I is currently vice-convenor of one committee and serves on a range of others including General Purposes, Property Services and Women's. She has previously held more senior posts and her experience of becoming a vice-convenor of a committee immediately on election is quite unusual – 'This was the first time the council had ever been Labour controlled and there was a big influx of new people including women and young people. It was a new administration, new people, people who didn't have experience. It was a very quick learning curve, but actually excellent to start off like that. You learn as you go along but it's really good, because it gives you the confidence and there is all the encouragement for you to take a position, I wasn't ever discouraged. Within two years I became convenor of that committee and then Secretary of the Labour group and then Leader of the then district council'. She lost her leadership position in the reorganisation to a unitary authority.

In addition Councillor I is on the Health Education Board for Scotland, is currently Vice-Chair of the Constituency Association, is the Association of Labour Councillors' representative and on the National Policy Forum of the Labour Party (representing councillors). In the past she has been on the Party's Scottish Executive representing councillors and on the NEC's local government committee. She was on the approved list of candidates for the Scottish parliament.

Councillor J

Female, age 67
First elected: 1978
Conservative councillor on a Scottish unitary council
Family circumstances: widowed
Education: Highers
Employment: retired

Councillor J had a keen interest in politics and local government and acted as election agent for her husband (who stood for the old town council and was later a councillor for the region) and for a number of other people. She stood for the district council and was elected in a by-election. She was encouraged to stand by the Conservative Party and was approached four or five times before she agreed. She did not want to stand whilst her husband was on the same authority. She eventually became a councillor on the district and he on the region.

Dealing with constituents is a high priority – 'It's good to know you can help somebody'. Her main interests include planning and culture. She is currently involved in a campaign to oppose building flats in an area of natural beauty. She has been involved in campaigning for or against many issues and is a well-known figure in the area. The effects of her campaigns against 'so-called art and theatre' have been mixed – whilst there has been some change in the direction she would wish, the coverage of herself in the media has frequently been unfavourable. However she feels that things have changed somewhat and two years ago one of the national newspapers wrote 'she has been right all along – filth is now masquerading as art'.

She is very keen on conservation and during her time as Convenor of the Cultural Committee saw a principal theatre refurbished and other important buildings upgraded. She feels that the refurbishment programmes are amongst her biggest achievements.

Her view on local government is that it has changed and is now about big business – 'That's not what local councils are about. It should be about caring about the city and people in the city. We have government and MPs to do the rest, with great big salaries. The thing is, to me it's got too political'.

Councillor J does not feel that being a councillor should be a full-time job – 'It's not like being an MP where you have to give up your life… It shouldn't be, it's what you make it. The only reason I'm so busy is that there are very few of us and some have to attend to business as they cannot afford to be completely dependent on council allowances… I'm of the old school – it should be a public service'.

She currently serves on a range of committees including education, finance and social work and is the spokesperson for one committee. In addition, she is currently vice-president of her own Conservative Association and Secretary of the Conservative Group on the city council. She has no other political ambitions.

Towards a Typology of 'Careers'

The results from our surveys, discussed in part in Chapter 4, would seem to provide some support for the idea that for some councillors at least, there is a growing relevance of the concept of a 'career'. This is illustrated by a range of evidence including the notion of progression to committee chair and other 'senior' posts within authorities, the continuing political ambitions of some councillors at both local and other levels, and perhaps most importantly by the clear emergence of 'full-time' councillors, particularly during the 1990s. The anecdotal evidence of several of the councillors portrayed above also suggests some support for such a view.

Councillors from Welsh unitary councils (59 per cent) were by far the least likely to have gone through a formal selection process. On all other types of council over 87 per cent (district councils) had had to undergo a formal selection process. This is likely to reflect the level of partisanship and participation by the main political parties in the different types of local government. Where the parties are less dominant there is more room for Independent and other self-selected candidates and councillors. Where parties dominate, the requirements for selection are more formal and, at least in theory, rigorous. However, it was only within the London boroughs and the metropolitan districts that respondents reported having experienced selection difficulties, usually as a result of competition or divisions within the local party. Only one respondent in England and Wales reported that they felt that they had experienced difficulty in selection arising from their being a woman. Only one-third of councillors in England and Wales and fewer than one in five in Scotland had fought a contest unsuccessfully prior to their election.

Building upon the discussion of full-time councillors in Chapter 4, Table 5.1 illustrates that there were significant variations across the different types of authorities with the old Scottish regions having by far the highest proportion of councillors describing themselves as full-time. Within England and Wales the higher proportions in the new unitary councils and the metropolitan districts might reflect both the demands of council work in those types of authority and the relatively recent elections – as pointed out in Chapter 4, there has been an apparently growing tendency for those elected during the 1990s to be more likely to be full-time councillors as soon as they take office. Whilst this might also be expected to hold true for the London boroughs they had last had elections in 1994 and they appear more likely to have meetings in the evenings, perhaps reducing somewhat the pressure on councillors to devote themselves full-time to council work.

Those who had been 'full-time' throughout their council career ranged from 2.5 per cent on district councils, 3.8 per cent on county councils, 7 per cent on metropolitan councils, 8.5 per cent on London boroughs and 10.3 per cent on Welsh unitaries to 12.5 per cent on English unitary councils. Whilst this is likely to be partly an artefact of the impact of the timing of the most recent elections for each type of authority, it also roughly reflects the position described above. In addition, as in Scotland, it appears that an increasing number of newly-elected councillors are undertaking the role 'full-time' immediately on election so that more than ten per cent of respondents from England and Wales had gone full-time since 1990.

Table 5.1 Full-time councillors by type of council, 1997

	Per cent
Scottish regions*	46.6
Scottish districts*	22.0
County councils	19.2
London boroughs	14.1
Metropolitan districts	24.0
English districts	10.5
English unitaries	23.4
Welsh unitaries	23.5

*Figures from 1996 survey of councillors in Scotland; weighted to correct gender balance.

From evidence such as this, together with the results presented in Chapter 4, it is possible to start to create a typology of councillors' 'careers'. This might range from those who stand for election through 'drifting' into candidature (Rao, 1998) and whose ambitions remain limited largely to 'backbench' council work, these being likely to be the great bulk of councillors, to the much smaller group who have much clearer political ambitions, whether these be focused primarily at the level of local government, or using this as one of the ways of moving onto the national stage. An initial very loose typology might therefore be conceived of along the following lines:

1) councillors who are largely content to do the work of a backbench councillor, but who might take on some additional responsibilities;

2) those who wish and seek to exert rather more influence, perhaps through chairing a committee;

3) those with further political ambitions, such as leading a party group or even a council;

4) those who see further political progression for themselves outside the council arena.

Of course, councillors' views of their 'careers' may not be settled and might vary considerably over time and with experience. They will also be affected by a wide variety of other factors such as their domestic situation, internal party politics and the necessity of being elected periodically. And this categorisation is based primarily upon councillors' *personal* ambitions, whilst party, political or other developments might mean that their careers might or might not 'progress' regardless of these. Nevertheless this would seem an appropriate starting point for future analysis of careers. These can also be used to relate to other classifications such as Newton's (1976). For example, Newton's *parochial* councillor might normally be content to follow the path in category 1) unless some unforeseen development should encourage them to develop a new 'career path'. Similarly, the association of the rise of 'municipal socialism' in the 1980s was sometimes equated with councillors who were *policy advocates* or *policy brokers*, both groups who might be expected to have greater political ambition, as illustrated by a number of Labour MPs such as David Blunkett and Ken Livingston who first came to prominence during this period. In addition, this development appears to have coincided with, and perhaps even was one of the causes of the increase in the number of full-time councillors. It would not be surprising if this type of councillor was more likely to commit themselves more completely to the role (and therefore to go 'full-time') and to have ambitions both within and outside local government. Similarly, the increasing amount of council work during the 1980s and 1990s and the greater opportunities for a reasonable level of remuneration might have served not only to bring new people with different attitudes into local government, but also to encourage some existing councillors to see potential for further progression.

Applying this to the case studies, there are clear examples fitting each of the categories. For example, Councillors B and G match well with 1), D with 2), C with 3) and H and I with 4). Some, such as Councillor A, might be seen as lying between two categories, in this instance 1) and 2).

The data from our surveys suggest that an increasing number of councillors are going 'full-time', including a significant proportion who have gone full-time from the date of their election. Eleven per cent of those in our sample for England and Wales had gone full-time since 1990. If this is correct and such a trend were to continue then it is possible that there may be significant pressure for change emerging from within local government.

The introduction of new forms and tiers of government by the Labour government may also serve to act as an encouragement for some to see politics as a career. The evidence from Scotland showed that two-fifths of respondents would have had some ambitions to stand for a Scottish parliament, and indeed, of the 129 MSPs elected in 1999 at least one-third had experience in local government, whilst 31 were councillors at the time of their election (SLGIU, 1999). Of those surveyed in England and Wales 31 per cent expressed some interest in standing for any regional assembly, should the opportunity arise, whilst 19 per cent said they would consider standing for the Westminster parliament and 14 per cent for the European parliament. Together with the evidence presented above and in Chapter 4, it would seem that the application of the concept of 'career' in elected local government may be becoming increasingly more apposite.

6 Comparative Perspectives

There has been little comparative work published on local government, and in particular on councillors, let alone when combined with analysis on the basis of gender or even party. Where there has been comparison it has tended to focus on the structure and functions of local government, with some attention paid to process (for example, Batley and Stoker, 1991; Chandler, 1993). There is of course, a sizeable literature on women in politics, but for many countries much of this focuses upon politics at the national level and in particular on the proportion of women in national legislatures (or other national institutions). This should not be dismissed, since there are lessons that can be learned and perhaps transferred, albeit with an awareness that there may be different circumstances and that conclusions may not always be appropriate to the local level. For example, in many countries there are significant differences in women's participation and experiences at national and local levels. Existing research can, however, be helpful as it is important to be aware of both different ways of approaching representation of women and even the notion of careers, as well as bringing an appreciation of the different ways in which countries operate. For example, one way in which women's contribution to legislation in Australia and the United States has been measured is in terms of the number of bills they introduce and the way in which they vote on issues (Considine and Deutchman, 1994); in Australia the influence of women has been measured by their role in the legislative process, as Cabinet members or through their work on parliamentary or party committees (Broughton and Zetlin, 1996, p. 51). These may certainly be valid approaches to measuring influence, although the extent to which they are sufficient even to those countries may be questioned, let alone their transferability to other states.

The Comparative Method

There is an extensive literature dealing with comparison in politics and public policy. Taken together this displays a considerable evolution of the comparative method, particularly over the last three decades, and in particular a shift away from comparative study based upon constitutions, to new forms of comparative analysis. Yet, there remains no universally agreed formula for comparative analysis. It is therefore important to cultivate an awareness that there remain a variety of very different approaches, and to be aware that each is likely to have limitations as well as advantages.

The principal benefits from comparison might be summarised as:

- the ability to set the experience of one country in the context of others;

- provision of useful insights into alternative arrangements;

- to allow a fuller understanding of the systems available in other countries;

whilst the shortcomings include:

- difficulties of language and culture;

- the interpretation of the experience of other countries in terms of one's own;

- the interpretation of social and political rules;

- the danger of taking cross cultural difference too far;

- difficulties in collecting and collating comparable data.

Despite agreement amongst many academics of the potential usefulness of comparative analysis there is no consensus over the best way to undertake such an approach and there are many pitfalls and problems. As highlighted above there is a need to be clear about the interpretation of social and political rules. For example, although most countries have local governments, the understanding of their role within national political structures may be very different. Similarly, it is necessary to exercise judgement about cross-cultural similarities and differences. Other problems are frequently compounded by a lack of available data on different countries; and even where this does exist it is rarely strictly comparable. In this context, for example, the *European Network 'Women in Decision-Making'* document notes the problems of collecting information in this field and that 'The compilation of the data must be considered accordingly' (Commission of the European Communities, 1992, p. 1) with the consequent caution that the figures within it should only be considered as an overview.

Yet despite the continuing weaknesses of the method, comparative research is potentially valuable as it might help to provide a fuller understanding of the experiences and 'careers' of councillors and the wider issues related to party, gender and local government, by setting the situation in the United Kingdom against the context of the position in other countries.

However, in addition to the methodological difficulties, the literature on councillors, and particularly women councillors, can perhaps best be described as sparse, with the exceptions of the United States and the United Kingdom. The material examined here is therefore highly heterogeneous taking very different approaches, with different foci and methods being used in different countries. Whilst the bulk of information comes from north western Europe and the United States, the inclusion of Japan and Poland serves to provide us with rather different perspectives.

There follows below a brief outline of the political structures and systems that operate in the countries most discussed in the remainder of this Chapter.

Japan

Japan is a unitary state in which the Diet (*Kokkai*) is the highest organisation of state power. This consists of the House of Councillors or *Sangi-in* (the Upper House) and the House of Representatives or *Shugi-in* (the Lower House). The term of a member of the House of Representatives is four years. All adults of Japanese nationality aged 20 or over have the right to vote. Female representation in the *Kokkai* peaked in the first post-war election in 1946 with 39 women in the *Shugi-in* and whilst the 1996 result saw 23 women winning seats (up from 14 in 1993) the level remains extremely low.

There are two tiers of local government: prefectures and municipalities. The prefectures deal with issues such as regional economic development and major public works which impact beyond a single municipality, as well as co-ordination of education standards, the police and state administration. The municipalities are responsible for hospitals, local health and welfare facilities, local public utilities and local environmental protection. Each prefecture has a directly elected assembly serving terms of four years and a governor also directly elected by the public. Governors and members of the prefectures receive a salary. There are 47 prefectures or administrative regions and over three thousand municipalities, including cities, towns and villages. Each municipality has its own autonomous local government with an elected mayor and assembly.

The powers and responsibilities of local government are delegated by central government. The powers of the municipalities are generally identical, other than a few larger cities which have designated status, with a consequent reduction in the powers of the prefecture over the region covered by those cities. Local government is overseen centrally by the Local Autonomy Ministry, and the power relationship has been structured in a manner which gives central government considerable power over local government.

Norway

Norway is the only Scandinavian country that retains a bicameral system. The *Storting* (Parliament) is at the top of the political structure. Beneath it local government consists of 19 counties and 435 municipalities. These are autonomous bodies run by directly elected officials (elected to the *fylkesting* in the case of the counties and the *kommunestyret* for the municipalities), although the independence of these bodies is limited by conditions, regulations and laws established by the *Storting*. Municipalities and counties operate at the same level and neither is subordinate to the other. Counties are responsible for provision such as secondary schools, hospitals and other special health services as well as county roads and transport; municipalities' responsibilities include child care, primary schools, general health services, social welfare, municipal roads and some aspects of public health provision. Unusually, Norwegian law states that local government can voluntarily take on additional responsibilities in any area that is not specifically defined as under the jurisdiction of another official body. However, despite this the post-war years have seen an increasing central control over local government. The local authorities are responsible between them for raising about one-fifth of the country's taxation. There are direct elections to the *kommunestyret* and to the *fylkesting*, with the period of office being four years. Norway is the only one of the Nordic countries where local government does not have constitutional protection.

At the national level the representation of women in Norway has risen steadily, particularly from the 1960s with the *Storting* having been over thirty per cent female during the 1990, whilst the 1980s and 1990s have seen campaigns to get more women involved in politics at all levels.

Poland

As one of the former Eastern bloc states Poland's post-war experience provides an interesting comparison in terms of both the political structure and the representation of candidates. In 1980 Solidarity, the first independent trade union to be established in a communist country was formed. In 1989 there were partially free elections and in 1990 the leader of Solidarity, Lech Walesa was elected president. The first fully free parliamentary elections took place in 1991 and again in 1993.

The Polish Parliament consists of the Senate (upper house) and the *Sejm* (lower house). Local government is based upon communes (*gmina*) consisting of local councils based in towns and villages. Local government was reformed before the first fully free local council elections in 1990, being given a greater degree of autonomy with the intention that this encourage a transition from a centralised economic and political system to one in which the various elements of local government were empowered to act for themselves. It is responsible for services such as arts and culture, education and housing. The 1997 constitution provides additional legal support for local self-government.

During the run up to the first entirely free parliamentary elections that took place in 1993 there were strong attempts by a number of women's organisations to achieve a greater representation of women in the Parliament. However, this was unsuccessful and led Siemienska to conclude that 'The election results once more confirmed the rule observed earlier in Poland that in a period of harsh political struggle women's representation decreases' (1994, p. 78).

Sweden

The Swedish Parliament, the *Riksdag*, is elected for a four year period by proportional representation. It is notable for the (relatively) large proportion of women members, with 41 per cent being female following the 1994 election. Below it lies local government which the Swedish constitution gives the right to levy taxes to fulfil its functions. Local government consists of the county council (*landsting*) as the regional unit and, at a more local level the municipality (*kommun*). The post-war years have seen a reduction in the number of municipalities through merger, falling from around two thousand to less than three hundred, whilst there are twenty-three county councils. The county councils are responsible for services which are seen as requiring a larger population base, such as medical and health care, as well as some of the personal social services, whilst the municipalities provide many services such as education, housing and leisure facilities. Almost one-third of public revenue comes from local taxation.

In the 1920s Stockholm introduced a system whereby city commissioners were paid on a full time basis, although other municipalities did not introduce similar systems until much later. In Sweden the need to employ certain full-time paid elected representatives has been attributed to the rapid expansion of the municipal administration and bureaucracy during the 1960s and 1970s. By the mid-1990s practically all municipalities had full-time elected representatives or commissioners, with a number of others being paid on a part-time basis.

Women are far better represented in politics than in most countries outside the Nordic area. The reasons for this are believed to include the high educational level and labour market participation rate of Swedish women, combined with other factors such as their legal entitlement to parental leave and the existence of municipal child and elder care systems.

According to Häggroth et al. (1996, pp. 103-4) '…Swedish municipal and county council politicians enjoy rather good working conditions…'. The guiding principle behind this has been that everyone should have an equal chance to accept and carry out local elected positions, and no one should have to pass up such a position for financial reasons. The Local Government Act obliges a municipal or county council to pay a reasonable level of compensation for any working income and social insurance benefits that an elected representative forfeits while he or she is performing council duties.

United States

In the USA the Federal Government sits at the top of the structure of government, consisting of the President, Senate and the House of Representatives. The tier beneath this is State government and at the base of the hierarchy there exists local government. Each State has the right to approve and alter parts of the structure and functioning of local government. Partly as a result of this there are a wide variety of forms 'local government'. Most states are subdivided into counties, with counties in turn divided into cities, towns and townships. However, Connecticut has no county governments and in Virginia the counties and cities are completely separate. Furthermore there are a huge variety of special district governments, ranging from water quality and local school districts, to transportation and airport authorities (Fesler and Kettl, 1996). Despite this diversity local governments can generally be categorised as having a major concern with the provision of goods (water, transport, electric and gas) and services (police and fire). They are also responsible for the administration of a broad range of other services including health, hospitals, parks and recreation.

Political systems vary widely, with many parts of local government being theoretically 'non-partisan', so that overt party competition can be relatively rare. Similarly, methods and remuneration of councillors varies widely, but elected mayors and councillors generally receive allowances. However, as in the United Kingdom, it is the case that some councillors do consider themselves as 'full-time'.

Women continue to be significantly under-represented at federal and state levels. By the mid-1990s only slightly over one-in ten members of the House of Representatives were women. In the lower houses of state legislatures the situation varied widely from only 5 per cent in Kentucky to 41 per cent in Washington, with the mean being 21 per cent (Darcy et al., 1994).

Socio-Economic Characteristics

As noted throughout this book, councillors in the United Kingdom tend to be sociologically unrepresentative of the population, being disproportionately male, middle-class, middle-aged, and educated to college or university standard. This is not unusual. Offerdal (1994) notes that middle aged white males are over-represented on municipal councils in Norway. This trend of under-representation of women in local government can also be found in Japan where, according to Takeyasu 'the fundamental trend in female participation in politics has continued basically unchanged for the past half a century...' (1997, p. 1). Her research, partly undertaken with Kasuga (1997), was grounded in a 'belief that women councillors may sometimes have different social backgrounds and motivations from men councillors' (Takeyasu, 1997, p. 3) and aimed to answer questions such as why there are so few women in Japanese politics? Of necessity this research commenced at a basic level because of the limited number of surveys or other studies undertaken in this field in Japan. However, the findings illustrate that male and female councillors do come from different social backgrounds. For example, male councillors had strong connections with their birthplace in that their 'supporter group' was largely based on a kinship and/or neighbourhood relationship. In contrast women were more likely to be 'independent' in that they were not affiliated to any particular party and their 'supporter group' was not made up of people from established organisations (Takeyasu, 1997). The father's employment was considered in terms of social background. In general, male councillors had a higher proportion of fathers who worked in sectors such as agriculture, forestry and fishing, in small factories or who were self-employed shopkeepers; women councillors had a higher proportion of fathers who worked in the public sector. Thus women come from a different social spectrum. In respect of education, male councillors were much more likely to have left education at primary and junior high school level whilst women councillors were much more likely to have left education at the junior and technical college level. The numbers going on to University were relatively similar overall although there were significant regional differences (Takeyasu, 1997).

In Poland women councillors are on average older than men, with the greatest proportion (42 per cent) being in the age group 40 to 49 whilst for men the largest age group is 30 to 39 to which 38 per cent belong. Women are more educated than men with 44 per cent having a University education compared to 28 per cent of men. The occupations of elected women include: teachers (28 per cent), individual farmers (16 per cent), doctors and nurses (12 per cent), clerks (9 per cent), economists (6 per cent) and technicians (6 per cent). Thus they work predominantly in specialist, managerial and non-manual occupations. In contrast, the largest group amongst men is farmers (32 per cent). Seven per cent are entrepreneurs (Siemienska, 1994).

Despite the decline in Polish women's representation in the post-Communist period Siemienska argues that 'the social characteristics of recently elected women make them more "real" politicians than was formerly the case. These women are better able to compete and discuss as skilled partners with male politicians' (1994, p. 87).

Survey evidence from the United States again provides a picture of socio-economically unrepresentative local political élites, with younger people, women, black people and those from manual occupations being less likely to be councillors (Eldersveld, 1995).

Numbers: Representation or Under-representation?

Given the limitations of comparative analysis and the available literature the remainder of this Chapter considers a number of issues relevant to women councillors and their 'careers', such as selection and election, representation and recruitment and socio-economic characteristics, drawing upon a variety of literature where it is available in these areas and for different countries. There is no particular rationale for the use of particular countries; those dealt with in any detail were selected primarily because there was literature available on local councillors which was relevant to this book.

The Commission of the European Communities document (1992) *European Network "Women in Decision-Making"* provides some baseline statistical data on the participation of women in political and public decision-making. Figures (see Table 6.1) on the participation of women at local political level range from 28 per cent in Denmark (1989) and 22 per cent in the Netherlands (1990) at the top end, to 9 per cent in Greece (1990) and 7 per cent in Luxembourg (1987) at the lower end. Whilst no figures were available for the UK in this publication, this compares with around one-fifth to one-quarter of councillors, depending upon the type of authority, although the figure is significantly lower in Northern Ireland where '...just 11.5 per cent of elected district councillors are women' (Lucy, 1994, p. 171, cited in Rallings and Thrasher, 1997a). For all EC Member States where data was available the average percentage of women local councillors was 19 per cent, approximately 8 per cent higher than the participation of women in parliamentary assemblies for all Member States (Commission of the European Communities, 1992).

Table 6.1 The participation of women at local political level, EC member states

	Date of election	No. councillors	No. women councillors	% women councillors
Belgium	1988	12,750	1,825	14.3
Denmark	1989	3,991	1,123	28.1
Germany	1990	No data	No data	No data
Greece	1990	5,654	507	9.0
Spain	1991	No data	No data	No data
France	1989	505,248	86,849	17.1
Ireland	1992	883	102	11.6
Italy	1990	99,705	9,222	9.2
Luxembourg	1987	880	62	7.0
The Netherlands	1990	10,359	2,279	22.0
Portugal	1989	7,796	789	9.9
United Kingdom	1988	No data	No data	No data
Total		546,211	102,758	18.8

Source: Commission of the European Communities (1992) *European Network "Women in Decision- Making"*, Commission of the European Communities, Brussels, p. 97.

In the United States, since the 1970s women's representation has gradually increased on local councils, in state legislatures and at executive branch level. Clark (1994) suggests that the steady growth of women's representation at all three levels of government reflects a number of developments, such as the rise of the women's movement being accompanied by greater political involvement by women, whilst Mueller (cited in Clark, 1994, p. 101) argues that it has '...increased the legitimacy of women's political ambition'. Clark also notes the tendency for women to achieve greater representation at the lower-level offices with the number of women on county and municipal boards tripling since 1975. However, such analyses obscure the fact that in practice there is huge variation between the fifty states in respect of women's representation at the municipal level. The

District of Columbia, Hawaii, and Michigan lead with the highest proportion of women in municipal office, with 50 per cent, 30 per cent and 28 per cent respectively, whilst Nebraska, Tennessee and Vermont have the lowest with 8 per cent, 7 per cent and 6 per cent respectively (Centre for the American Woman and Politics, National Information Bank on Women in Public Office, cited in Clark, 1994, pp. 102-4).

In many United States cities overt partisan conflict is largely absent, with fewer than one-third of cities with populations of two thousand five hundred or more having charters which provide for partisan government (Eldersveld, 1995). Historically partisan government for cities has been disliked by many reformers who have linked it to the situation at the turn of the century when local party 'machines' were seen as corrupt, inefficient, and detrimental to community development.

According to Kasuga (1997, p. 1) in 1996 there were almost sixty-five thousand local councillors in Japan and just over four per cent of these were women. He points out that it would appear that the main element of Japanese women's political participation consists of voting rather than actually standing for election or becoming a councillor. This can be illustrated by the following argument: Japanese women were given equal voting rights to men in 1945, they were also given the right to stand for Parliament and in local elections. Up until 1950 the turnout of men at elections was greater than that for women, however from 1955 the turnout of women in some big towns and cities has begun to outstrip men, and this trend has continued (Kasuga, 1997). Kasuga does not explore the reasons for this trend but notes that it is not possible to develop a theoretical basis for women's political participation because so little survey research has been undertaken on Japanese women councillors.

In Norway the representation of women is significant. They have a strong presence in the Cabinet and throughout the country's national and local governments. For example, at the end of 1989, women made up 36 per cent of the members of the *Storting* (Parliament), 41 per cent of the representatives on the county councils, 31 per cent on the municipal councils, 33 per cent of the members of national boards and committees and 36 per cent of the members of municipal boards and committees (Kelber, 1994, p. 82). Following the 1993 election 39 per cent of the *Storting* was female, although this fell back to 36 per cent in 1997. By 1995 women held 33 per cent of seats on municipal councils and 41 per cent of seats on counties. These figures are not only higher than in many other countries, but illustrate that there are equal or greater proportions of women holding higher level offices than lower level, although they are still under-represented compared with men.

In Sweden women hold greater numbers of posts at local level than at national level, although the difference between them is eight per cent or less. The proportion of women elected representatives has increased since the 1960s to the position in the 1994 election where they accounted for 41 per cent of municipal council seats and 48 per cent of county council seats Häggroth et al. argue that 'Men nevertheless dominate the executive committee and the committees with technical specialities. Women are primarily found in 'soft' specialities such as cultural affairs and social welfare' (1996, pp. 102-3).

In Poland the local council elections held in 1990 were the first fully free elections in Polish post-war history. Women constituted 15 per cent of candidates and 11 per cent of elected councillors, resulting in fewer women in local government than had been the case under Communism. Siemienska believes that this supports 'the thesis that there is a relationship between an increase of political tension and a decrease in the presence of women in politics' (1994, p. 80) with this being further borne out by the results of Parliamentary elections in 1989 and 1991.

Explaining Women's Under-representation

Many of the explanations, largely from Britain and the United States, have previously been considered in Chapter 3 and so are not dealt with here in any detail.

The local political electoral system in Japan is characterised by a masculine culture and this positively influences the election of male candidates. The behavioural patterns in collecting votes particularly in rural and urban-rural areas where traditionally male candidates and councillors have inherited seats from their predecessors, is cited by Kasuga (1994) as a contributing factor in explaining women's under-representation in local councils. Because women are disadvantaged by this process Kasuga suggests that among the alternatives open to women might be: to campaign like men, on what he terms a 'fundamental relationship' basis, for example on the basis of blood ties, ties by marriage and neighbourhood organisations (for many at present, this is also linked with support from the dominant Liberal Democratic Party); to get support from progressive parties such as the Japan Communist Party, Japan Socialist Party; or to get support from voluntary groups (network relations and supporter groups). However, he suggests that prospects for changes in party policy on women's representation in Japan are slim Kasuga (1997) and that it is likely to take several decades before these occur.

In Chapter 3 the desirability thesis was put forward as a partial explanation of women's under-representation in local (and national) politics in the UK and the USA. However data from other countries, such as Norway and Poland do not appear to bear this out. To recap, the 'desirability thesis' holds that '…the probability of women being elected to public office varies inversely with the power and prestige of those offices' (Engstrom, McDonald and Chou, 1988, p. 38). Siemienska (1994) refers to this as the 'power-pyramid hypothesis' and illustrates that in Poland women's representation in local politics tends to be at higher levels than men's. So, for example, women are more likely to be elected in towns and cities (the intermediate level of local politics) than in villages. A number of different explanations are given for this such as the persistence of traditional attitudes at the local (lowest) level and the lower level of formal education of women than men in rural areas.

This presents an interesting contrast with women's representation in countries such as the UK and the USA. It is clearly difficult to arrive at any answer as to why women's representation is at a higher level in the 'power-pyramid' in Poland, but it is possible that in addition to cultural influences the role of political parties might be important, whilst the role of trade unions in the recruitment process and in providing valuable political experience may also have an influence.

In Norway, the gradual increase in women in elected politics stretches back to a Labour government's (1965) plans to implement a '…United Nations recommendation that all countries should develop their own plans of action to solve the problems facing women' (Kelber, 1994, p. 66). The government therefore sought to increase the number of women elected to local councils, including by the establishment of a campaign committee led by the Prime Minister and a former Prime Minister. All the political parties were represented on the committee, as were the main women's organisations. They promoted an educational campaign through the media and public schools that '…stressed the valuable contribution of women to politics…' (Kelber, 1994, p. 66). According to Kelber (1994) the success of Norwegian women in gaining political power can therefore be attributed to three factors: firstly, well organised political campaigns; secondly, the strategy of reordering the placement of candidates on local ballots to facilitate the election of women, resulting in substantial gains for women in the 1967 local council and 1971 national elections, although after this electoral laws were changed to make the use of this procedure more difficult; and thirdly, the use of quotas by political parties in recruitment and election procedures and in appointments to public committees, boards and councils. The latter were incorporated into the Equal Status Act, Section 21 of which was amended in 1988 'to mandate at least forty per cent representation of both sexes on committees, boards and councils appointed or elected by a public agency or institution' (Kelber, 1994, p. 81). This is diligently enforced by the *Ombud*. Whilst this does not wholly explain why women are represented in equal or greater numbers at higher levels of government than they are at local level, it does suggest that government support, and party involvement, particularly in creating a culture where women were seen as valuable assets in politics, may be an important factor.

Several of the main political parties have also adopted quota rules, which Sundberg (1995) argues 'had a larger effect on the political culture around parties than any other single decision to promote female representation. By raising quotas within the party organisation, it forces the male members to reflect on gender proportions in any public assembly where candidates are nominated or elected, regardless of whether quota rules are formalised in them or not' (p. 107).

In the Nordic countries women's representation is generally stronger at the national level than at the local level. Raaum (1995b) makes the point that in Norway 'Larger municipalities meant more women councillors. Much in the same vein, central control on the part of political parties in the process of candidate selection enhances women's chances to gain office' (p. 279). One of the results of this is that as Raaum (1995a) points out, the 'iron law of andrarchy', that the disproportionate advantage of male, educated, high-status élite recruits increases the higher up the power structure we move, may not fit well with the position in the Nordic countries, and that a 'lag hypothesis' may be more appropriate, as the relative under-representation of women may decline over time.

Remuneration

Remuneration of local government representatives is one area where there is little information available. What there is suggests that there is a very mixed picture both between and within countries. The Swedish Local Government Act allows elected representatives a variety of benefits including compensation for loss of earnings, pensions and holiday benefits. However, it also allows each council to determine both levels of compensation and whether representatives should be remunerated 'for the work which their mandate entails', together with a pension and other financial benefits. Those who 'discharge their mandates full time or for a considerable proportion of full time' (who are salaried) are excluded from these arrangements. This phenomenon has become much more common from the 1960s and 1970s and most municipalities and all county councils have at least one full-time elected representative or commissioner (*kommunalråd*) whilst medium and larger areas may have ten to twenty. These commissioners often hold the most important chairs on the executive committees and specialist committees, whilst opposition commissioners may be full-time but do not have responsibilities for local government operations (Häggroth et al., 1996).

Whilst little information is available on Japan the governor and members of assemblies of prefectures are all paid, normally at a level somewhat below that of members of the Diet but well above the average for local government employees.

In the United States the pattern varies considerably so that in some areas councillors can receive a salary, whilst in others they are limited to remuneration for expenses. Similarly, in Canada most councillors serve on a part-time basis, with compensation for loss of earnings and some with greater responsibilities receiving additional allowances. However, some larger municipalities pay salaries to their leaders who can then commit themselves to their position full-time (Chandler, 1993).

Overall the position appears similar to that reported for the Widdecombe Report (1986b) with many states offering 'financial payment or compensation to council members. The arrangements vary between and within nations, and between types of council office' (p. 142).

Turnover

There is again little evidence available on the turnover of councillors. Offerdal (1994) looks at the high turnover rate amongst Norwegian councillors (around 65 per cent) and comments on the selection process, noting that 'the main reason for the high turnover rate is related to self-selection rather than to selection... Councillors themselves simply do not want re-election' (Offerdal, 1994, p. 5). Amongst the reasons given for this were the conflict between council work and home life, mentioned by around forty per cent of councillors, in addition between ten and fifteen per cent gave reasons such as their lack of influence in council, a dissatisfaction with their performance in council, loss of income and party squabbles (Offerdal, 1994). Kerley (1992) has examined the turnover of local councillors in Scotland. His findings, and those of Bloch (1992) in England and Wales have similarities with those of Offerdal in respect of the operation of a self-selection process whereby councillors chose not to stand again. Reasons cited for this were personal reasons such as age, length of service and ill health as well as the competing demands of work and family, also mentioned by Offerdal's respondents. Rallings and Thrasher (1997, p. 79) note that for England the turnover rate varies between around one-third and half of councillors across the country depending on the particular authority, and that the biggest reason for this turnover was 'voluntary resignation'.

Trends in Local Government Representation

This brief review has illustrated that there is a wide range of experience in different countries. As in the UK, there is evidence that local councils tend to be sociologically unrepresentative, containing a larger proportion of (middle class) men than the populations as a whole. The representation of women varies both within and between countries, with some states (including Norway, Poland and some USA states) having significant numbers of women in local politics. There is general agreement that a number of factors have frequently worked against the equal representation of women. These include responsibilities for caring and domestic work, problems of access to resources such as money, time and contacts, and conscious or unconscious discrimination by selectors and voters. A variety of explanations and suggestions for improving the representation of women are put forward in the various countries. These range from suggestions that women may have to change the way that they operate in Japanese local politics to the partial explanation provided by the 'desirability thesis' in the UK and the USA. However, the latter appears to fail as an explanatory tool when applied to Norway and Poland, perhaps reflecting that there is no cross-national and cross-state explanation for the differential representation of women in local government. In some states, particularly the Nordic countries, systems such as quotas for women candidates, methods of selection and forms of proportional representation (Matland, 1995) tend to have been seen as working in favour of greater representation of women. In addition, studies in both Norway and the UK highlight the fact that turnover of local councillors appears to operate largely on the basis of a self-selection process whereby local councillors opt not to stand again.

The increasing role of parties in local government also appears to be a common phenomenon across countries, with most councillors needing or using the party label and support to be elected. Chapters 4 and 5 have illustrated the apparent trend towards more full-time councillors in the United Kingdom. Whilst the evidence is scarce, and sometimes mixed, it is clear that in some other countries there has also been a continued trend towards the 'professionalisation' of local government representation, frequently allied with payments/forms of remuneration. This is most marked at the 'higher' levels of local government, with leaders or their equivalents being significantly more likely to be 'salaried' and to devote themselves to their position on a full-time basis. It is also more likely to occur in larger rather than smaller authorities. The evidence for extent to which the use of the term 'career' is appropriate in anything other than a fairly basic political sense (using election to local government to increase influence or perhaps to move towards representation at a higher political level) is therefore still unclear.

On a related but somewhat different issue Offerdal (1993) has suggested that in Norway the use of the term 'conscription' rather than 'career' might be appropriate for many councillors. This is because of the very high level of turnover (often approaching two-thirds) of local government councillors at each election. In addition the parties there are significant difficulties in finding people to stand for election and many have to be strongly encouraged. He identifies an 'A-team' who generally run the council (often the mayor and other members of the executive board) and a 'B-team' of backbench councillors or 'ordinary citizens… for whom council membership amounts to conscription' (p. 14).

Finally, it seems that there are a number of issues which are effectively common to the states covered in this research. Notable amongst these are the themes of recruitment and election, and in particular the role of political parties, representativeness and unrepresentativeness, and what can loosely be described as 'careers' (which might include remuneration, workload and turnover) following election. These may perhaps provide some groundings for future comparative work in this area.

7 The Future for Councillors

This book has sought to draw upon a variety of evidence loosely based around a very general notion of a council 'career', reflecting a number of factors such as the process of selection and election, potential progression to more influential or senior roles on a council, and the possibilities of council service being one route to a political career, either within local government or for some serving as a stepping stone to a national level. At the same time the book is also grounded in the different motivations, experiences and ambitions of female and male candidates and councillors. Our conclusions can therefore be summarised under four broad, often overlapping, themes: the role of political parties in local government; the continuing under-representation of women councillors; the impact of recent and possible future changes to the structure and management of local government; and the appropriateness or otherwise of further use of the concept of councillors' 'careers'.

The Role of Parties

The twentieth century saw a continual growth in the politicisation of local government so that by the late 1990s it was only in the most rural and outlying areas of the United Kingdom where the influence of political parties were not the dominant factor in local elections and local politics. This has had a number of impacts including increasing competition for seats, so that there are both more candidates and fewer councillors are returned unopposed, and has resulted in parties being the basis for much of the decision-making structure and process within local government. Rallings and Thrasher (1997a) analyse the issues associated with the electoral role of parties in some detail.

The rise of parties in local government also has a variety of implications for the key ideas underpinning this book. Among these are the recruitment patterns of potential councillors. One area of interest is the 'benign' influence of party which has in recent years arguably served to increase the number of women candidates and councillors. As parties have increasingly adopted (for whatever reasons) targets for women's representation and in some instances selection procedures designed to achieve these, so the proportion of women in elected positions has increased. This has been most notable at the national level, where Labour's temporary use of all-women shortlists resulted in a very significant increase in the proportion of women MPs at Westminster in 1997. Similarly, attempts by Labour (and the SNP in Scotland) to achieve near gender equality in the Scottish Parliament and National Assembly for Wales in 1999 meant that following the elections more than one-third of each body was made up of women. At local level it is also true that the parties have a higher proportion of women candidates and councillors than is found amongst Independents, but the recent improvement at national level has been much more dramatic.

In terms of selection the research undertaken for this book produces a rather different picture from that which has sometimes been suggested. In particular, the results of our surveys suggest that in many areas the requirement for previous party activity before selection for a potential council seat may be less than has been suggested by some other studies. Previous studies have suggested that for Labour activists in particular, party experience was an important factor in the selection process, yet relatively few of our respondents reported any difficulties in being selected as candidates and a significant number were actively encouraged to stand by the parties.

Particularly from the 1960s the role of party in local government has been recognised by central government and this has become insitutionalised in the structures and operation of decision-making processes. Labour's reforms pose significant questions about local democracy and accountability and the functions and responsibilities of council members in terms of both executive and representative roles. Not only are these important in themselves but as Brooks (1999) and Rao (1998) suggest, they have significant implications for the future recruitment of potential councillors in terms of the powers and functions of local government, the constraints of individuals' workloads and the continuing dominance of party in candidate selection and the operation of councils.

The Under-Representation of Women

There is a powerful argument that local elections and local government in general offer more favourable conditions for women to become actively involved in politics than is the case in national politics. Yet it remains the case that only around one-quarter of local councillors are women and the biggest increases in the proportions of elected women in recent years have been at the national level.

There have been many explanations put forward for the continuing under-representation of women, and a variety of possible methods of categorising these. Broadly these can be described as those which focus on the circumstances and characteristics of individuals and those which emphasise structural or societal explanations. In terms of representation at local government level it seems likely that many of these have considerable validity and that to some extent it is the cumulative impact of a variety of influences that contribute to the current position. Yet it is also the case that the past two decades have seen a slow but steady increase in the proportion of candidates and councillors who are women. At the same time Rao (1998) notes that socio-economic change has also been eroding the one advantage which at least some women have had in the past – the time to participate in community and political affairs – with women increasingly likely to be in work whilst also taking on the major burden of domestic responsibilities.

Importantly perhaps, there is little or no evidence that voters discriminate against women candidates. Yet despite this it remains true that women are not competing on an equal footing with their male counterparts. For example, party selection processes are often dominated by men who may not be well-disposed to choosing women for the most winnable seats, and the burden of contesting an election and serving as a councillor may be too great for many women so that when they do stand they are often fighting unwinnable seats. Whatever the reason the outcomes are the same and women candidates are less likely to be found contesting the most winnable seats. Rallings and Thrasher (1997a) suggest that it may therefore be necessary to reconsider the way that elected local government works and that 'At the very least being a councillor needs to be seen as like any other occupation with elected members paid and given the necessary administrative and technical support to fulfil their functions properly' (p. 78).

Finally, it should be noted here that it might also be appropriate to undertake a similar analysis for people from ethnic minorities, but their relatively small numbers and the lack of comprehensive data makes this a significantly more difficult task.

Changes to the Structure and Management of Local Government

The changes to the structure and operation of local government made under the Conservatives from 1979 to 1997 have not reduced the pressure for further reforms under Labour. From the time of their election the Blair government has paid considerable attention to what it has viewed as problems or deficiencies in local government including accountability, democracy and decision-making processes. The role of councillors has not been exempt from this. The white paper *Modern Local Government: In Touch with the People* (DETR, 1998b) stressed issues such as accountability, responsiveness and representativeness. It proposed consideration of changes to the electoral system, reforms to the decision-making structures of local government, a 'new ethical framework' and a variety of strategies to improve participation.

Many of these changes not only affect the role of councillors but also have significant links with the idea of careers in local government. In early 1999 the Labour government announced plans for the first systematic training programmes for local councillors, when the Education and Employment Secretary David Blunkett proposed to set up a nationwide scheme to send over four thousand elected members on courses to improve their knowledge of what councils should do to raise standards in education (*The Guardian*, 7 January 1999). In contrast, the introduction of cabinet-style local government and elected mayors serves to underline the distinction between frontbench or executive councillors and their backbench colleagues.

In Scotland the establishment of the Scottish Parliament from 1999 added a further complication to the relationship between central and local government. The Commission on Local Government and the Scottish Parliament was established to examine this and came up with wide-ranging and far-reaching recommendations including the use of proportional representation for local government elections. Although this was of necessity specific to Scotland the work of the Commission perhaps inevitably reflected concurrent developments and debates in England and Wales and much of its argument is of relevance to local government in general. Among it's considerations those most relevant to the current study included that 'Everything we have been told, in our visits and consultations, including by many councillors themselves, points to the conclusion that the present situation in Scotland is unsatisfactory and in need of review' (1998, p. 24) and that 'It is little wonder then that being a councillor in Scotland is now generally regarded as a full-time job' (1998, p. 24). However, whilst the Commission accepted that it might always be necessary for some councillors to be full-time, when taking on executive responsibilities, they suggested that 'too many members of the community are excluded from the possibility of standing for council election. That in turn impoverishes councils by depriving them of talents and experience. It also makes for less representative councils' (pp. 24-5). In their *Consultation Paper 2* they considered whether employers should be encouraged, or even compelled, to grant career breaks or secondments to employees who get elected to a council. Alternatively they considered whether council business could be reorganised so that members' workloads would not be incompatible with other occupations. The final report (CLGSP, 1999) in many ways provided a summary of much current thinking on local government and made a number of recommendations relevant to councillors' careers including:

- councils should review their political decision-making;
- that this should include the organisation of council business to enable a wider cross-section of the community to consider taking on the responsibilities of council membership;
- all councils should produce a job description for members;
- a pay and conditions package should be drawn up with remuneration of councillors subject to independent review;
- consideration should be given to the provision and resourcing for member training and personal development.

'Careers'

Labour's reforms of local government in England and Wales and Scotland in many respects make the notion of council careers increasingly appropriate, with such emphases as those on education and training for councillors, improved decision-making processes and elected mayors. Yet the position voiced by the Commission on Local Government and the Scottish Parliament (1999) still remains strong:

> ...the normal expectation should be that council membership should be compatible with full-time employment or another full-time occupation, and that... it would seem logical to retain the concept of a basic allowance, which does not purport to be a salary but offers some reasonable recompense for what is in fact voluntary service. [But] For those members who carry the heaviest responsibilities, for example as leader or member or an executive group, leader or an opposition group or equivalent position, there should be a reasonable salary commensurate with their responsibilities.
>
> Commission on Local Government and the Scottish Parliament (1999) *Moving Forward: Local Government and the Scottish Parliament*, Scottish Office, Edinburgh, p. 33.

This suggests that despite the widely recognised substantial workloads of many council members and the apparent growth in the number of full-time councillors the prospect of an officially recognised large proportion of salaried councillors remains slight. There are also a number of other questions around the recruitment and retention of councillors. People become councillors for a wide variety of reasons – some drift into it or are encouraged by others to stand for election, usually building upon other forms of local or community involvement, some enter local politics for personal satisfaction, whilst others have strong political beliefs which they wish to act upon. Similarly, councillors display widely varying ambition – some are content to act as backbench councillors, fulfilling the representative role and Newton's (1976) parochial function. Others wish to exercise greater influence on policy issues within their authorities, either through chairing committees or through progressing to positions such as council leader. And a proportion either enter local politics with, or later develop, clear ambitions for a political career, which may remain within local government or which might progress to a wider stage.

The evidence presented in this book suggests that there is at the least a strong case for the consideration of the council membership of many councillors in terms of a 'career', if not in the sense of a job, in recognition of the existence of political careers, whether remaining within local government or moving on to other elected office. It seems probable that the early years of the twenty-first century will see the further development of a variety of forms of political structures within local councils, such as directly elected mayors (or provosts), cabinets and executives. This is likely to mean a redistribution of power and responsibility among councillors, increasing the degree of 'professionalisation' which has been evident since the 1980s. In addition, other possible developments, such as the potential use of proportional representation, will have an impact on councillors. It seems likely, therefore, that the use of the term 'career' will become still more appropriate over the next decade.

Bibliography

Adonis, A. (1990), *Parliament Today*, Manchester University Press, Manchester.

Arblaster, A. (1987), *Democracy*, Open University Press, Milton Keynes.

Bains, M. (Chairman) (1972), *The New Local Authorities: Management and Structure*, HMSO, London.

Barron, J., Crawley, G. and Wood, T. (1987), *Married to the Council? The Private Costs of Public Service*, Department of Economics and Social Science, Bristol Polytechnic.

Barry, J. (1991), *The Women's Movement and Local Politics*, Avebury, Aldershot.

Batley, R. and Stoker, G. (eds) (1991), *Local Government in Europe: Trends and Developments*, Macmillan, London.

Birch, A.H. (1972), *Representation*, Macmillan, London.

Bledsoe, T. and Herring, M. (1990), 'Victims of Circumstances: Women in Pursuit of Political Office', *American Political Science Review*, vol. 84, pp. 213-23.

Bloch, A. (1992), *The Turnover of Local Councillors*, Joseph Rowntree Foundation, York.

Blondel, J. (1990), *Comparative Government: An Introduction*, Philip Allan, London.

Bochel, H.M. and Denver, D.T. (1994), *Scottish Regional Elections 1994: Results and Statistics*, Election Studies, Dundee.

Bochel, H.M. and Denver, D.T. (1995), *Scottish Council Election 1995: Results and Statistics*, Election Studies, Newport on Tay: Fife.

Bochel, J.M. and Denver, D.T. (1983), 'Candidate Selection in the Labour Party: What the Selectors Seek?', *British Journal of Political Science*, vol. 13, pp. 45-69.

Bochel, J.M. and Denver, D.T. (1992), *Scottish District Elections 1992: Results and Statistics*, Election Studies, Dundee.

Boddy, M. and Fudge, C. (eds) (1984), *Local Socialism*, Macmillan, London.

Boles, J.K. (1989), 'Images of Female and Male Elected Officials: The Effect of Gender and Other Respondent Characteristics', *Journal of Political Science*, vol. 17, pp. 19-31

Bristow, S.L. (1980), 'Women Councillors: An Explanation of the Under-Representation of Women in Local Government', *Local Government Studies*, vol. 6, pp. 73-90.

Brooks, J. (1999), '(Can) Modern Local Government (be) in touch with the people?', *Public Policy and Administration*, vol. 14, pp. 42-59.

Broughton, S. and Zetlin, D. (1996), 'Queensland ALP Women Parliamentarians: Women in Suits and Boys in Factions', *International Review of Women and Leadership Special Issue: Women and Politics*, vol. 2, pp. 47-61.

Brown, A. (1995), *Legislative Recruitment in Scotland: The Implications for Women of a New Parliament*, Paper presented to the ECPR Joint Sessions, 27 April to 2 May, Bordeaux.

Brown, A. (1996), 'Women and Scottish Politics', in Brown, A., McCrone, D. and Paterson, L. (eds) *Politics and Society in Scotland*, Macmillan, Basingstoke, pp. 163-88.

Brown, C. (1994), 'Judgements about the Capabilities of City Councillors and Support for Female Representation on City Council', *Social Science Journal*, vol. 31, pp. 355-73.

Brown, C., Heighberger, N.R. and Shocket, P.A. (1993), 'Gender-Based Differences in Perceptions of Male and Female City Council Candidates', *Women and Politics*, vol. 13, pp. 1-17.

Bullock, C.S. and MacManus, S.A. (1991), 'Municipal Electoral Structure and the Election of Councilwomen', *Journal of Politics*, vol. 53, pp. 75-89.

Butler, J. and Scott, J.W. (eds) (1992), *Feminists Theorize The Political*, Routledge, London.

Cadwallader, M. (1995), 'Councillors in Wales', *Local Government Studies*, vol. 21, pp. 376-95.

Carroll, S. J. (1985), 'Political Elites and Sex Differences in Political Ambition: A Reconsideration', *Journal of Politics*, vol. 47, pp. 1231-43.

Chandler, J.A. (ed.) (1993), *Local Government in Liberal Democracies: An Introductory Survey*, Routledge, London.

Chandler, J. A. (1996), *Local Government Today*, Manchester University Press, Manchester.

Clark, J. (1994), 'Getting There: Women in Political Office' in Githens, M., Norris, P. and Lovenduski, J. (eds), *Different Roles, Different Voices: Women and Politics in the United States and Europe*, Harper Collins, New York, pp. 99-110.

Cochrane, A. (1993), *Whatever Happened to Local Government?*, Open University Press, Buckingham.

Commission of the European Communities (1992), European Network "*Women in Decision- Making*" Commission of the European Communities, Brussels.

Commission on Local Government and the Scottish Parliament (1998), *Consultation Paper 2*, The Stationery Office, Edinburgh.

Commission on Local Government and the Scottish Parliament (1999), *Moving Forward: Local Government and the Scottish Parliament*, Scottish Office, Edinburgh.

Considine, M. and Deutchman, I.E. (1994), 'The Gendering of Political Institutions: A Comparison of American and Australian State Legislators', *Social Science Quarterly*, vol. 75, pp. 854-66.

Convention of Scottish Local Authorities (1996), *Advice to the New Councils 3: Special Responsibility Allowances*, CoSLA, Edinburgh.

Cooper, C.L. and Davidson, M. (1982), 'The High Cost of Stress on Women Managers', *Organizational Dynamics*, vol. 10, pp. 44-53.

Costantini, E. (1990), 'Political Women and Political Ambition: Closing the Gender Gap', *American Journal of Political Science*, vol. 34, pp. 741-70.

Crewe, I., Sarlvik, B. and Alt, J. (1977), 'Partisan Dealignment in Britain, 1964-1974', *British Journal of Political Science*, vol. 7, pp. 129-90.

Dalton, R. and Knechler, M. (eds) (1990), *Challenging the Political Order*, Polity, Oxford.

Darcy, R. (1992), 'Electoral Barriers to Women', in Rule, W. and Zimmerman, J. F. (eds), *United States Electoral Systems: Their Impact on Women and Minorities*, Greenwood Press, Westport: Connecticut, pp. 221-32.

Darcy, R., Welch, S. and Clark, J. (1994), *Women, Elections and Representation*, University of Nebraska Press, Lincoln: Nebraska.

Davidson, M. and Cooper, C.L. (1984) 'Occupational Stress in Female Managers: A Comparative Study', *Journal of Management Studies*, vol. 21, pp. 185-205.

Department of the Environment (1983), *Streamlining the Cities*, HMSO, London.

Department of the Environment (1989), *The Internal Management of Local Authorities in England*, Department of the Environment, London.

Department of the Environment, Transport and the Regions (1998a), *Modernising Local Government: Local Democracy and Community Leadership*, DETR, London.

Department of the Environment, Transport and the Regions (1998b) *Modern Local Government: In Touch with the People*, The Stationery Office, London.

Derr, C.B. (1986), *Managing the New Careerist*, Jossey Bass, San Francisco.

Diamond, I. (1977), *Sex Roles in the State House*, Yale University Press, New Haven.

Duke, L.L. (ed.) (1996), *Women in Politics: Outsiders or Insiders?*, Prentice Hall, Upper Saddle River: New Jersey.

Elcock, H. (1986) *Local Government: Politicians, Professionals and the Public in Local Authorities*, Methuen, London.

Elcock, H. (1994), *Local Government: Policy and Management in Local Authorities*, Routledge, London.

Eldersveld, S.J. (1995), *Party Conflict and Community Development*, University of Michigan Press, Ann Arbor.

Eldersveld, S.J., Stromberg, L. and Derksen, W. (1995), *Local Elites in Western Democracies*, Westview Press, San Francisco.

Elzar, D.J. (1972), *American Federalism: A View from the States*, Thomas Y. Crowell, New York.

Engstrom, R.L., McDonald, M.D. and Chou, B. (1988), 'The Desirability Hypothesis and the Election of Women to City Councils: A Research Note', *State and Local Government Review*, no. 20, pp. 38-40.

Farrell, D.M., Broughton, D., Denver, D. and Fisher, J. (eds) (1996), *British Elections and Parties Yearbook 1996*, Frank Cass, London.

Fesler, J.W. and Kettl, D.F. (1996),*The Politics of the Administrative Process*, Chatham House, New Jersey.

Fox, D.M. (1974), *The Politics of City and State Bureaucracy*, Goodyear Publishing, Pacific Palisades: California.

Galloway, K. and Robertson, J. (1991), 'Introduction: A Woman's Claim of Right for Scotland', in Woman's Claim of Right Group, *A Woman's Claim of Right in Scotland: Women, Representation and Politics*, Polygon, Edinburgh, pp. 1-6.

Grant, J. (1993), *Fundamental Feminism*, Routledge, London.

Gray, A. and Jenkins, W. (1994), 'Local Government', in Jones, B., Gray, A., Kavanagh, D., Moran, M., Norton, P., and Seldon, A. (eds), *Politics UK*, Harvester Wheatsheaf, Hemel Hempstead, pp. 447-77.

Gray, C. (1994), *Government Beyond the Centre: Sub-National Politics in Britain*, Macmillan, London.

Gyford, J. (1985), *The Politics of Local Socialism*, Allen and Unwin, London.

Gyford, J., Leach, S. and Game, C. (1989), *The Changing Politics of Local Government*, Unwin Hyman, London.

Häggroth, S., Kronvall, K., Riberdahl, C. and Rudebeck, K. (1996), *Swedish Local Government: Traditions and Reforms*, Swedish Institute, Stockholm.

Hakim, C. (1996), *Key Issues in Women's Work*, Athlone Press, London.

Hallett, C. (ed.) (1996), *Women and Social Policy*, Prentice Hall/Harvester Wheatsheaf, Hemel Hempstead.

Hampton, W. (1991), *Local Government and Urban Politics*, Longman, London.

Hayek, F.A. (1973), *Law, Legislation and Liberty*, Vol. III, Routledge and Kegan Paul, London.

Hayes, B.C. and McAllister, I. (1996), 'Political Outcomes, Women's Legislative Rights and Devolution in Scotland', in Farrell, D.M., Broughton, D., Denver, D. and Fisher, J. (eds) *British Elections and Parties Yearbook 1996*, Frank Cass, London, pp. 143-57.

Herr, E.L. (1990), 'Issues in Career Research', in Young, R.A. and Borgen, W. A. (eds), *Methodological Approaches to the Study of Career*, Praeger, New York, pp.1-21.

Heywood, A. (1994), *Political Ideas and Concepts: An Introduction*, Macmillan, London.

Hill, D.B. (1981), 'Political Culture and Female Political Representation', *Journal of Politics*, vol. 43, pp. 159-68.

Hills, J. (1982), 'Women Local Councillors: A Reply to Bristow', *Local Government Studies*, vol. 8, pp. 61-71.

Hills, J. (1983), 'Life-Style Constraints on Formal Political Participation: Why so few Women Local Councillors in Britain?', *Electoral Studies*, vol. 2, pp. 39-52.

Hollis, P. (1989), *Ladies Elect: Women in English Local Government, 1865-1914*, Clarendon Press, London.

Jenkins Commission (1998), *Report of the Independent Commission on the Voting System*, The Stationery Office, London.

John, P. (1990), *Recent Trends in Central-Local Relations*, Joseph Rowntree Foundation, York.

Karnig, A.K. and Walter, B.O. (1976), 'Election of Women to City Councils', *Social Science Quarterly*, no. 56, pp. 605-13.

Karvonen, L. and Selle, P. (eds) (1995), *Women in Nordic Politics: Closing the Gap*, Dartmouth, Aldershot.

Kasuga, M. (1997), 'Local Councillors in Modern Japan: Considerations on Some Sociological Differences Between Men and Women Councillors', Paper presented at the Tenth Biennial Conference of Japanese Studies Association of Australia, University of Melbourne, 8 July 1997.

Kavanagh, D. (1996), *British Politics: Continuities and Change*, Oxford University Press, Oxford.

Keith-Lucas, B. (1977), *English Local Government in the Nineteenth and Twentieth Centuries*, The Historical Association, London.

Kelber, M. (ed.) (1994), *Women and Government: New Ways to Political Power*, Praeger, Westport.

Kerley, R. (1992), *Changing the Guard: A Study of Councillor Retiral and Replacement on Scotland's Island and Regional Councils*, Scottish Local Authorities Management Centre, Glasgow.

Leach, R. (1996), *British Political Ideologies*, Prentice Hall, Hemel Hempstead.

Leach, S., Stewart, J. and Walsh, K. (1994), *The Changing Organisation and Management of Local Government*, Macmillan, Basingstoke.

Lindsay, I. (1991), 'Constitutional Change and the Gender Deficit', in Woman's Claim of Right Group, *A Woman's Claim of Right in Scotland: Women, Representation and Politics*, Polygon, Edinburgh, pp. 7-13.

Lipsky, M. (1979), *Street Level Bureaucracy*, Russell Sage Foundation, New York.

Lively, J. (1975), *Democracy*, Basil Blackwell, London.

Local Government Management Board (1997), *Survey of Local Authority Councillors 1997*, LGMB, London.

Long, B.C. and Kahn, S.E. (1990), 'A Structural Model Approach to Occupational Stress Theory and Women's Careers', in Young, R.A. and

Borgen, W.A. (eds), *Methodological Approaches to the Study of Career*, Praeger, New York, pp. 235-43.

Lovenduski, J. (1993), 'Introduction: the Dynamics of Gender and Party', in Lovenduski, J. and Norris, P. (eds), *Gender and Party Politics*, Sage, London, pp. 1-15.

Lovenduski, J. and Norris, P. (eds) (1993), *Gender and Party Politics*, Sage, London.

Lovenduski, J. and Norris, P. (eds) (1996), *Women in Politics*, Oxford University Press, Oxford.

Lucy, G. (1994), *Northern Ireland: Local Government Election Results*, 1993, Ulster Society Publications, Armagh.

MacManus, S.A. and Bullock, C.S. (1989), 'Women on Southern City Councils: A Decade of Change', *Journal of Political Science*, vol. 12, pp. 32-49.

MacManus, S.A. and Bullock, C.S. (1992), 'Electing Women to City Council: A Focus on Small Cities in Florida', in Rule, W. and Zimmerman, J.F. (eds), *United States Electoral Systems: Their Impact on Women and Minorities*, Greenwood Press, Westport: Connecticut.

MacManus, S.A. and Bullock, C.S. (1996), 'Second Best? Women Mayors and Council Members: A New Test of the Desirability Thesis?', in Duke, L.L. (ed.), *Women in Politics: Outsiders or Insiders?*, Prentice Hall, Upper Saddle River: New Jersey.

Martlew, C., Forrester, C. and Buchanan, G. (1985), 'Activism and Office: Women and Local Government in Scotland', *Local Government Studies*, vol. 11, pp. 47-65.

Matland, R. (1995), 'How the Election System Structure has Helped Women Close the Representation Gap', in Karvonen, L. and Selle, P. (eds), *Women in Nordic Politics: Closing the Gap*, Dartmouth, Aldershot, pp. 281-309.

Maud, Sir John (Chairman) (1967), *Committee on the Management of Local Government, vol. 1: Report*, HMSO, London.

Mezey, S.G. (1980), 'The Effects of Sex on Recruitment: Connecticut Local Offices', in Stewart, D.W. (ed.), *Women in Local Politics*, Scarecrow Press, Metuchen: New Jersey, pp. 61-85.

Miliband, R. (1982) *Capitalist Democracy in Britain*, Oxford University Press, Oxford.

Newton, K. (1976), *Second City Politics*, Clarendon Press, Oxford.

Norris, P. and Lovenduski, J. (1995), *Political Recruitment: Gender, Race and Class in the British Parliament*, Cambridge University Press, Cambridge.

Offerdal, A. (1994), 'Career or Conscription: Recruitment of Norwegian Local Councillors', Paper prepared for the workshop on local government in Norway and France, Talence, Centre d'Etude et de Recherche sur la Vie Locale, 4-5 November 1993 (revised draft 6. 11. 94).

Parry, G., Moyser, G. and Day, N. (1992), *Political Participation and Democracy in Britain*, Cambridge University Press, Cambridge.

Pascall, G. (1986), *Social Policy: A New Feminist Analysis*, Routledge, London.

Petersson, O. (1994), *The Government and Politics of the Nordic Countries*, Fritzes, Stockholm.

Pitkin, H.F. (1972), *The Concept of Representation*, University of California Press, London.

Pryde, G.S. (1960), *Central and Local Government in Scotland Since 1707*, Routledge and Kegan Paul/The Historical Association, London.

Raaum, N. C. (1995a), 'The Political Representation of Women: A Bird's Eye View', in Karvonen, L. and Selle, P. (eds), *Women in Nordic Politics: Closing the Gap*, Dartmouth, Aldershot, pp. 25-55.

Raaum, N.C. (1995b), 'Women in Local Democracy', in Karvonen, L. and Selle, P. (eds), *Women in Nordic Politics: Closing the Gap*, Dartmouth, Aldershot, pp. 249-280.

Rallings, C. and Thrasher, M. (eds) (1993), *Local Elections in Britain: A Statistical Digest*, Local Government Chronicle Elections Centre, Plymouth.

Rallings, C. and Thrasher, M. (1997a), *Local Elections in Britain*, Routledge, London.

Rallings, C. and Thrasher, M. (1997b), *Local Elections Handbook 1997*, Local Government Chronicle Elections Centre, Plymouth.

Rao, N. (1998), 'The Recruitment of Representatives in British Local Government: Pathways and Barriers', *Policy & Politics*, vol. 26, pp. 291-305.

Rasmussen, J. (1983), 'The Electoral Costs of being a Woman in the 1979 British General Election', *Comparative Politics*, vol. 18, pp. 446-75.

Redcliffe-Maud, Lord (Chairman) (1969), *Royal Commission on Local Government in England, 1966-1969, vol. I Report*, HMSO, London.

Rhodes, R. (1992), 'Local Government', in Jones, B. and Robbins, L. (eds), *Two Decades in British Politics*, Manchester University Press, Manchester, p. 205-18.

Roberts, G. and Edwards, A. (1991), *A New Dictionary of Political Analysis*, Edward Arnold, London.

Robinson, C. (Chairman) (1977), *Remuneration of Councillors: Vol I: Report; Vol II: The Surveys of Councillors and Local Authorities*, HMSO, London.

Rule, W. and Zimmerman, J.F. (eds) (1992), *United States Electoral Systems: Their Impact on Women and Minorities*, Greenwood Press, Westport: Connecticut.

Rush, M. (1969), *The Selection of Parliamentary Candidates*, Nelson, London.

Scholzman, K.L., Burns, N. and Verba, S. (1994), 'Gender and the Pathways to Participation: The Role of Resources', *Journal of Politics*, vol. 56, pp. 963-90.

Scott, A. (1990), *Ideology and the New Social Movements*, Unwin Hyman, London.

Scottish Local Government Information Unit (1990), 'New Allowances Fail to Satisfy', *Scottish Local Government*, 31, July/August, 1990.

Scottish Local Government Information Unit (1995a), *The Guide to Scottish Local Government*, SLGIU, Glasgow.

Scottish Local Government Information Unit (1995b), 'Scotland's Councillors: A Profile', *Scottish Local Government*, 75, August 1995.

Scottish Local Government Information Unit (1999), 'The 1999 Scottish Elections', *Scottish Local Government Information Unit Bulletin*, 113, May/June 1999.

Scottish Office (1998a), *The Commission on Local Government and The Scottish Parliament: Consultation Paper 1*, The Stationery Office, London.

Scottish Office (1998b), *The Commission on Local Government and The Scottish Parliament: Consultation Paper 2*, The Stationery Office, London.

Seltzer, R., Newman, J. and Leighton, M.V. (1997), *Sex as a Political Variable: Women as Candidates and Voters in US Elections*, Lynne Rienner, Boulder: Colorado.

Sharp, C. (1991), 'Women Councillors', in Woman's Claim of Right Group, *A Woman's Claim of Right in Scotland: Women, Representation and Politics*, Polygon, Edinburgh, pp. 34-46.

Shaul, M.S. (1982), 'The Status of Women in Local Governments: An International Assessment', *Public Administration Review*, vol. 42, pp. 491-500.

Siemienska, R. (1994), 'Women in the Period of Systematic Changes in Poland', *Journal of Women's History*, vol. 5, pp. 70-89.

Squires, J. (1996), 'Quotas for Women: Fair Representation?', in Lovenduski, J. and Norris, P. (eds), *Women in Politics*, Oxford University Press, Oxford, pp. 73-90.

Stewart, D.W. (ed.) (1980), *Women in Local Politics*, Scarecrow Press, Metuchen, New Jersey.

Stewart, J. (1995), 'The Internal Management of Local Authorities', in Stewart, J. and Stoker, G. (eds), *Local Government in the 1990s*, Macmillan, Basingstoke, pp. 69-85.

Stewart, J. and Stoker, G. (1995), 'Fifteen Years of Local Government Restructuring, 1979-1994: An Evaluation', in Stewart, J. and Stoker, G. (eds), *Local Government in the 1990s*, Macmillan, Basingstoke, pp. 69-85.

Stewart, J. and Stoker, G. (eds) (1995), *Local Government in the 1990s*, Macmillan, Basingstoke.

Studlar, D.T. and Welch, S. (1987), 'Understanding the Iron Law of Andrarchy: Effects of Candidate Gender on Voting in Scotland', *Comparative Political Studies*, vol. 20, pp. 174-91.

Studlar, D.T. and Welch, S. (1991), 'Does District Magnitude Matter? Women Candidates in London Local Elections', *Western Political Quarterly*, vol. 44, pp. 457-66.

Studlar, D.T. and Welch, S. (1992), 'The Party System and the Representation of Women in English Metropolitan Boroughs', *Electoral Studies*, vol. 11, pp. 62-9.

Sundberg, J. (1995) 'Women in Scandinavian Party Organizations', in Karvonen, L. and Selle, P. (eds), *Women in Nordic Politics: Closing the Gap*, Dartmouth, Aldershot, pp. 83-111.

Takeyasu, H. (1997), 'Local Councillors in Modern Japan: Women Councillors after World War II', Paper presented at the Tenth Biennial Conference of Japanese Studies Association of Australia, University of Melbourne, 8 July 1997.

Tullock, G. (ed.) (1976), *The Vote Motive*, Institute of Economic Affairs, London.

Tullock, G. (1988), *Wealth, Poverty and Politics*, Basil Blackwell, Oxford.

Vallance, E. (1979), *Women in the House: A Study of Women Members of Parliament*, Athlone Press, London.

Walby, S. (1986), *Patriarchy at Work*, Polity Press, Cambridge.

Welch, S. (1985), *Why Women Aren't Elected to Office: Some British and American Comparisons*, Paper presented to the 13th World Congress of the International Political Studies Association, July 15-20, Paris.

Welch, S. and Karnig, A.K. (1979), 'Correlates of Female Office Holding in City Politics', *Journal of Politics*, no. 41, pp. 478-91.

Welch, S. and Studlar, D T. (1988), 'The Effects of Candidate Gender on Voting for Local Office in England', *British Journal of Political Science*, vol. 18, pp. 273-81.

Wheatley, Lord (Chairman) (1969), *Royal Commission on Local Government in Scotland*, Report, HMSO, Edinburgh.

Widdecombe, D. (Chairman) (1986a), *The Conduct of Local Authority Business*, HMSO, London.

Widdecombe, D. (Chairman) (1986b), *The Conduct of Local Authority Business: Research Volume II: The Local Government Councillor*, HMSO, London.

Widdecombe, D. (Chairman) (1986c), *The Conduct of Local Authority Business: Research Volume II: Aspects of Local Democracy*, HMSO, London.

Wilford, R., Miller, R., Bell, Y. and Donoghue, F. (1993), 'In Their Own Voices: Women Councillors in Northern Ireland', *Public Administration*, vol. 71, pp. 341-55.

Woman's Claim of Right Group (1991), *A Woman's Claim of Right in Scotland: Women, Representation and Politics*, Polygon, Edinburgh.

Working Party on the Internal Management of Local Authorities (1993), *Community Leadership and Representation: Unlocking the Potential*, HMSO, London.

Young, K. and Rao, N. (1994), *Coming to Terms with Change? The Local Government Councillor in 1993*, Joseph Rowntree Foundation/LGC Communications, London.

Young, R.A. and Borgen, W.A. (eds) (1990), *Methodological Approaches to the Study of Career*, Praeger, New York.

Zimmerman, J.F. (1992), 'Fair Representation for Minorities and Women', in Rule, W. and Zimmerman, J.F. (eds), *United States Electoral Systems: Their Impact on Women and Minorities*, Greenwood Press, Westport: Connecticut, pp. 3-11.

Index